WHY CAN'T
THEY SEE ME?

WHY CAN'T THEY SEE ME?

My Sister Jan's Story

SAM ANTRIM KANE

iUniverse, Inc.
Bloomington

Why Can't They See Me?
My Sister Jan's Story

iUniverse books may be ordered through booksellers or by contacting:

iUniverse
1663 Liberty Drive
Bloomington, IN 47403
www.iuniverse.com
1-800-Authors (1-800-288-4677)

ISBN: 978-1-4759-4344-3 (sc)
ISBN: 978-1-4759-4343-6 (hc)
ISBN: 978-1-4759-4342-9 (ebk)

Library of Congress Control Number: 2012914546

Printed in the United States of America

iUniverse rev. date: 09/25/2012

Jan was the utmost Olympic winner
because of all the hurdles she jumped throughout
her life.

Averill McCullough

CONTENTS

ACKNOWLEDGEMENTS

When I began writing this book, I realized I needed a hand to facilitate finishing it.

I give thanks to my mom, Ruby Kane, for editing and adding her contribution to this book.

I also bestow gratitude on my sister Linda Duncan for her input into this book and her help to Mom at this difficult time in our lives.

Jan was great at keeping journals, records and memoirs of things throughout her life, and I commend her for it. Some of her chronicles even included where she and Mom stopped for gas when traveling—Jan loved to travel. Some of the information in this book came from her journals, because some of the things she recorded must have been important to her.

And to Mom's friend Averill McCullough my deepest appreciation for her thoughtful insight into my sister when she said, "Jan was the utmost Olympic winner because of all the hurdles she jumped throughout her life."

INTRODUCTION

This is a chronicle about my sister Jan. I am dedicating this book to all who have a physical difference, special people, and people who are disadvantaged. You will see that those who have dissimilarities can be strong and determined and can persevere against incredible odds. They can become successful, and enjoy life regardless of how we treat them. I also want those who feel remorseful for the disadvantaged to understand that we make life more difficult for them by gawking, bullying, criticizing, showing disapproval, and thinking they are not normal, when in actuality they may be more intelligent than the average person. Looks do not tell the story.

I have written this story in memory of my sister Jan. I wanted her to write this because she would have said so much more than I ever could. All Jan ever wanted was to be treated as an equal; and to be given an opportunity by people to know her heart, not just what they saw. We claim to be different in America and to be: charitable, caring people. Maybe we should reevaluate our lives and give everyone the opportunity to be whoever he or she is.

* * *

Our mom, Ruby Jones, was one of eight children born on a farm. She was the third child and the only daughter. Our dad, Murray Kane, was a World War II veteran. He tried college but decided he wanted to farm his grandfather's farm near Murray, Iowa.

Mom had just turned eighteen. She most likely wanted to go to college and become a registered nurse before she got married and started a family, but I believe that our entire destiny is God's purpose and we are to live according to what God wants for us.

*   *   *

Jan was born in 1955 with Riley-Day syndrome, now known as Familial dysautonomia. Familial dysautonomia is a malfunction of the autonomic nervous system which effects the development and survival of some neurons in the autonomic and sensory system resulting in variable symptoms.

Symptoms displayed by a baby with Familial dysautonomia might be the absence of overflow tears after age seven months; this symptom can be dramatically obvious due to bilateral eye irritation; and weak or absent sucking instinct or misdirected swallowing which may be caused by a weak swallowing tone.

Symptoms in an older child with FD includes: delayed speech and walking, unsteady gait, corneal abrasions, poor growth, less pain perception, inability to produce tears, poor growth, unstable, and fluctuating blood pressure. People with FD have frequent episodes of pneumonia, problems with speech, movement, difficulty swallowing, and inappropriate perception of heat, pain, and taste. FD does not affect intelligence. Jan was born with all of these symptoms.

Dysautonomia was originally reported by Conrad Milton Riley and Richard Lawrence Day in 1949. According to the Dysautonomia Foundation death occurs in fifty percent of affected individuals by age thirty. Jan was fifty-two when she passed on.

After Jan died in 2007, I made a mask out of fabric, cutting slits in it for my eyes. I put plastic over the slits and tied the mask around my head. I imagined this was what Jan was able to see. When I looked through the mask, I could not see more than about fifteen feet and then not clearly. My heart really went out to my sister even more. I had not comprehended how bad her vision really was.

Even though Jan had her ups and downs, hard times and good times, bad habits, and caring ways, I believe God gave her to us for a purpose.

I know that she accepted God before she died and will someday be resurrected as perfect as the day she was born.

If God gives saint-hoods, truly my sister will receive one for all she endured and overcame in her life. Jan went to sleep in blessed hope of Christ's return and the resurrection.

CHAPTER 1

Welcome to the Family

Grandpa Jones had rented a 120-acre farm next to my dad's farm, and my uncles attended to the cattle and crops-on the rented farm. They became acquainted with my dad, Murray Kane. My uncles liked the rodeo and asked my dad if he would like to go with them. He said he would. Mom had planned to go with them, but her brothers didn't want her to go since my dad was going. Grandpa and Grandma told the boys that their sister had been planning on going to this rodeo as long as they had, and they needed to let her to go with them. So Don, Cliff, Morris, Mom, and Murray went to the rodeo. Mom and Dad rode in the back seat going home and Dad sang "Ruby" from the 1952 movie *"Ruby Gentry"*. They all had a memorable time.

One day, when my uncles were working on Grandpa's property, Dad told Uncle Cliff to ask Mom if she would go out with him. Cliff told him to ask her himself, so he told Cliff to tell her he would be over at 7:00 p.m. on Saturday night. Cliff was always teasing and joshing Mom so when he told her what Dad had said, she didn't believe him. On Saturday night, Cliff told Mom she better get dressed, as Murray would be coming to take her out. She still did not believe him, but Grandpa told her to get dressed and if Murray did not show up then Cliff would get a whipping. Mom got dressed, and Dad showed up at 7:00 p.m.

Mom worked at the Clarke County Hospital as a nursing assistant. Dad would sometimes pick her up at work, and they would go to a movie. When she had a day off, they would sometimes visit Dad's Uncle Vernon in Creston, Iowa. Dad liked to dance and taught Mom to waltz. They dated about six months before Dad asked Mom to marry him.

They were married on my grandparent Kane's' anniversary, Christmas Eve 1953. They were married in the parsonage of the Methodist Church in Murray, Iowa. The ceremony was performed by Reverend Lacy Thompson. Mom's brother, John and his wife, Phyllis were the best man and matron of honor. Mom had been maid of honor at their wedding. Mom's friend Ruth sang "Because" and was accompanied on the piano by Cheri, one of Mom's classmates. The reception, attended by both families, was at Dad's grandma and grandpa's home in Murray, Iowa. When everyone went out to see the bride and groom off and to wish them a Merry Christmas, one of the candles on a table caught the table cloth on fire. Luckily, someone went back in to get something and was able to put the fire out. What a way to finalize a wedding.

Mom did not drive and she thought it was too much for Dad to get up take her to work and then pick her up after work, so she quit her job at the hospital and helped Dad on the farm. She planted a garden every summer and canned some of the fruits and vegetables. They had plum and apple trees, so she made use of them. Later on, they bought a freezer so she could freeze some of the fruits, vegetables, and some meat. She also helped Dad with loading the baled hay and putting it into the barn. Since the house was not modern and was without running water and bathrooms, she had to heat the water for laundry in a large galvanized tub and then dump it into the washer. Drinking water had to be carried to the house in a bucket. Mom raised chickens and butchered them for cooking and freezing. Dad thought she should learn to drive, so he taught her to drive a stick-shift 1951 Plymouth.

They had been married five months when Mom became pregnant. Dad's cousin Larry White, who was in the military, came to visit, and apparently Mom's manner fluctuated from sweet and friendly to depressed and grouchy. Dad could not understand what her problem was.

Larry told dad, "She's pregnant".

After Larry left, Dad told Mom what Larry had said. She had thought she might be pregnant but had not said anything to Dad because she wasn't sure. She waited a couple of months and then made an appointment with Dr. George who acknowledged she was pregnant. They did not have pregnancy tests in those days, so women had to wait until the doctor could hear the fetal heart-beat. The pregnancy went well. Mom never had morning sickness, and the depressed grouch disappeared.

My sister Jan was born around 2:30 p.m. on Saturday, February 19, 1955. She was a perfect little twenty-one inch six pound-six ounce baby girl, with not a blemish or imperfection what-so ever. Since Mom had worked at the hospital as a nursing assistant before getting married, the nurse in the labor and delivery department announce over the loud-speaker that Ruby had had a baby girl. Mom's parents were in the lobby waiting for the great happening, but little did they know it would be announced over the loud-speaker.

*   *   *

Baby Jan seemed in good health. She took a breath and cried as soon as she was delivered, but she didn't nurse very well that week in the hospital and lost weight to five pounds nine ounces before going home. Even after going home she would not nurse. One night Mom gave her a bottle and she took it. That did it Mom decided to put her on the bottle instead of nursing her. That was probably the only bottle she ever took without having to be coaxed and encouraged to eat.

There had been some debate about what to name her. Dad wanted to name her Jan but my parents could not think of a middle name to go with Jan. They finally came up with Janet Lucille. Dad did not like nicknames even though his family called him Bud, so he always called my sister Janet while everyone else called her Jan, which is the name she liked.

Uncle Tom was seven years old when Jan was born, and Uncle David was three. Uncle Dave thought she was perfect, just like Mom's dolls he played with. But Uncle Tom thought she should at least be able to walk. They loved Jan, as did the older uncles, John, Don, Cliff, Morris, and Gene. Uncle Tom and Uncle David being nearer her age loved having her to play with.

Nonnie, Dad's mother, came to stay with them for a week to do cooking, housework, laundry, and what-ever needed to be done. She couldn't understand why the baby didn't eat. Grandma Jones couldn't understand it either. She had seven boys and Mom and had never had a baby that wouldn't eat. Jan was drinking from a sippy cup at two months. They were so poor that Mom couldn't afford baby food, so she began feeding Jan Jell-O, pureed fruits and vegetables, and cream of wheat by the time she was three months old.

Jan could not lift and control her head until she was ten months old. Shortly after learning to control her head, she learned to sit up. And, at a year, she began scooting around and crawling. She could pull herself up and climb on things at about fifteen months, but could not walk until she was twenty-two months old.

*   *   *

Farming was hard work but Dad and Mom were managing. They were up early in the morning with Mom taking care of a new baby and making breakfast while Dad milked the cows and fed the hogs. Then after breakfast Dad was off to the field to plant corn or oats, mow the alfalfa and do what-ever else there was to do. Farm equipment in the 1950's was a lot slower than it is today. Instead of the machinery plowing ten rows as they do today, the machinery plowed one row at a time. Tractors were four cylinders instead of the big four-wheel drive diesels of today.

My dad knew nothing about farming when he moved to Great-Grandpa Kane's farm before he and Mom were married. Great-Grandpa was eighty-four-years old, and he had planned to teach Dad how to farm with horses. Great-Grandpa had an accident and broke his hip, so he was unable to be on the farm to train Dad. And as a result the neighbor, Myron Coon, taught Dad to farm with a Ford tractor. After Mom and Dad were married, Mom's family helped out as much as they could on the farm, but they had their own farm and both of Mom's parents had jobs. My Grandpa Kane wanted Dad to sell the farm and go to school or get a job. Grandpa Jones and Myron Coon tried to teach Dad how to get as much out of his farm as he could.

I was born February 11, 1956 on Grandma and Grandpa Jones's twenty-fourth wedding anniversary. Dad was the last of the male Kane's. Now, he had a farm-hand to carry on his Kane name, an Irish-man. Dad was proud of his Irish ancestry and named me Sam after Great-Grandpa Samuel Parker Kane and gave me a middle name of an Irish town: Antrim. Dad was a favorite of the great-grandparents, possibly because my grandpa Kane was like an only child (he had one sister who died in infancy) or possibly because Grandpa had worked at a bank during the Great Depression and, when the banks had failed, they'd lost everything. There had been no jobs and no money. So the family had moved in with my great-grandparents, and they had helped raise my dad and Aunt Marilyn.

*　　*　　*

Mom and Dad were sensing changes in Jan when she was about fourteen months of age. She was clumsy and rubbing her eyes a lot. She developed something that looked like mucus on the cornea of her left eye, but when Mom tried to clean it off, it did not move. Jan was referred to the University of Iowa Hospital in Iowa City, where she was diagnosed as having no blink reflex or tears, which dried her eyes out and caused her to develop an ulcer on the cornea of her left eye. The ophthalmologist surgically removed the ulcer and sewed Jan's' eye partially shut so it would not dry out and cause the ulcer to get worse. He put a patch over her eye for protection. They kept her in the hospital for a week and referred her to the pediatric department for neurological exams.

Mom stayed in the room with her, because by this time, Jan had learned to climb out of her bed and she needed to be watched. The nurses would pin a sheet over the top of her crib, but she would manage to crawl out. It became evident she did not have the ability to chew. She would wallow her food around in her mouth until it was soft enough to swallow. She was diagnosed as having Riley-Day syndrome. This disease is wide spread among Jews, but we had no Jews in our family that could be found. This was also a disease that infants were born with, and most children with Riley-Day do not live beyond the teen years because it affects all organs: lungs, kidneys, bladder, colon, vision, liver, and others. The doctors did not think Jan would live to be a teenager.

Jan's vision was affected to the degree of legal blindness, although Mom and Dad were not told this until she was eighteen years old. She made no tears until age three, but even then they were not of sufficient quantity to keep her eyes from drying out and itching. In 1970, a renowned Riley-Day doctor at Mercy Hospital in San Diego, California, tested Jan and determined she did not have the true Riley-Day syndrome, but suffered from something very similar, now known as dysautonomia syndrome. He said physical indications revealed she had Riley-Day: the lack of pain sensation, thin tight lips, inability to hold her head up at the usual age, no sucking instinct, etc. But the tests, seventy two hour urine test and blood tests were only slightly indicative and not at a level for a true diagnosis of Riley-Day.

*   *   *

Mom and Dad did all they could to protect infant Jan from rubbing her eyes. She kept taking the patch off and rubbing her eyes until some of the stitches came out. Then it was back to the University of Iowa Hospital. This time, they sewed her eye closed and splinted both arms so she could not bend them to rub her eyes. It meant a constant watch for Mom, especially when she took the splints off so Jan could feed herself. Jan would work at trying to take the splints off. She went to the University of Iowa every two weeks, then every month, then every three months, then every six months, then finally once a year. After four years, this came to a halt. The doctors had done all they could. Jan's eye was healed. They opened her left eye half way before she got into school. It stayed that way until she was twelve years old, when Mom opened it all the way, but the scarring caused her eyes to look asymmetrical.

Jan was growing and she was a curious little girl. She had not learned to walk yet, but most likely after my birth, she was trying to understand this new little person who had entered into her life. She always wanted to help Mom take care of me. She would pull herself up and put her hand through the crib rail and touch me or sit in the recliner chair beside Mom when she was holding me or feeding me.

She learned to walk after I learned to walk. I was ten months old, and she was twenty-two months. Her vision was 20/150, which meant that what a person with normal vision could see at 150 feet, Jan had to be at 20 feet to see it. Because of her vision, when learning to walk she would reach for a chair and miss it by six inches and hit her head on the chair or the floor. Later in life her vision was 20/200.

Mom was pregnant with Linda, but she and Jan made many trips by train to University of Iowa during the winter months. Mom was a very bashful girl growing up with two older brothers who protected her. Riding on the train and sitting with strangers helped this twenty-year-old grow up and become a friendly, sociable person.

During the summer, Dad would drive Mom and Jan to the Iowa City, which was 170 miles away. Cars did not go very fast, so they would get up in the morning and leave at 6:00 and arrive around 10:30 a.m. for their appointment and, then return home when they were finished. My uncles would do Dad's farm chores so he could leave early and return late.

Linda was born on February 17, 1957. Now, Jan and I had a new little person to play with. While Linda and I were too young to understand all that was happening with Jan, I'm sure Mom and Dad were very anxious as a result of all this. Their daughter was in poor health, and they had two other babies to worry about. Grandma Jones or Nonnie (Grandma Kane) would look after Linda and me when Mom was away with Jan. Their trips were long and tiring. They had faith in the University Hospital doctors, but they were confused as to what had caused this defect. To this day Dad doesn't understand. Mom has somewhat of a better understanding being a nurse and contacting the Dysautonomia Foundation to learn more.

CHAPTER 2

The Risks of Determination

Jan was a real Houdini from the time she could crawl. She would climb out of her high chair, out of the crib, up on the back of the sofa, on the washer, and on the oven door, and she would do everything except swing from the drapes. Mom had taken a cake-decorating class and had decorated a cake with roses on top and all around it. She was going to take it to the last-day-of-school picnic for her little brothers. She did not want Jan to get a hold of the cake, so she put it up on the second shelf above the washing machine in the pantry. The next morning, while Mom was feeding the chickens, Jan climbed up on a chair and then onto the washer and up onto the shelf above the washer. She reached up and picked all the flowers from around the cake. Mom was heart broken, but she rescued what she could and redecorated the cake and took it to the picnic.

Mom always took crayons and coloring books to church to keep us busy and quiet. One time in church, Jan was restless and would not be quiet. She kept talking and squirming. Mom had not heard one word the pastor had said. She took Jan out behind the church and paddled her. When church was over, Dad told Mom she had made a positive impact on the pastor's sermon. It was Mother's Day weekend, and he was talking about mothers' love. Mom had shown her love to Jan with discipline.

Linda was eighteen months old and Mom decided it was time to get a job to help out. Hog prices and corn prices had dropped, and most farmwomen had to work in order for the farmer to make it. At first Dad was opposed but knew it had to be. Mom had worked as a nurse's aide before marrying Dad, so she went back to work at the hospital. She loved her work but could make more money working at a factory. There was a clothing manufacturing company in Osceola known as Snowdon's. Several of our neighbors worked there. It was the main factory, if not the only one, in town. In those days, farmers' wives were like illegal immigrants of today, hard workers and cheap labor. Mom quit the hospital and went to work at Snowdon's for one dollar an hour. She had been making seventy-five cents an hour at the hospital.

It was hard work taking care of a farm. Everyone who could helped out. Our neighbors to the west, Blanche and Myron, would help. Myron would help bale the hay, and Dad would help him back. Blanche would watch Jan, Linda, and I while Mom worked and the men baled hay and worked in the fields. The Jones grandparents had jobs, but they and their sons helped when they could. And eighty-eight-year-old Great-Grandpa Kane helped when he could and with what he could do.

*   *   *

Jan always copied whatever Linda and I did, even though it seemed Jan was accident prone due to her vision, poor balance and poor coordination. One time on the farm, we were playing in the east barn hayloft. The barn was full of hay, making it hard to climb up the ladder. We climbed up the ladder and then had to climb on the hay bales to get into the hayloft. All at once Jan fell flat on her face about sixteen-feet down to the barn floor. There was blood all over, and it seemed as though she were lifeless. I was frightened and ran for Dad and Mom. They came running, because they knew with Jan these kinds of accidents could happen. Mom picked her up and stopped the bleeding. They took her to the hospital in Osceola and thank God she was all right. She seemed to be like a cat with nine lives.

Dad built a bar in our yard for us to drop from, kind of a gym-master bar. Jan would twirl over that bar, never falling. Dad also put a swing up in the old maple tree and Jan would swing and swing. One time, she swung so high that it frightened me. Then she fell flat on her face. She wasn't hurt, but no one ever really knew when she was hurt, because pain never affected her the way it did everybody else. At least she had no broken bones.

Mom had an old crank-wringer washer that she replaced with a new wringer washer. The washer was electric, but you had to put the clothes through the wringer instead of the machine spin-drying the clothes the way modern washing machines do. Some-how, Jan got her arm stuck in the wringer clear up to her armpit. Her curiosity apparently had gotten the best of her. Mom ran into the pantry where the washer was, unplugged the washer, and then opened the wringer so Jan could get her arm out. The underside of Jan's upper arm and muscle were injured. Her skin had large abrasions and bruises from the elbow to her armpit. Jan wound up with a pretty bad scar on the under-side of her upper arm.

Mom wanted to ice skate on the pond. She bought herself and each of us kids ice skates. Mom made colored pompoms to put on the laces of Jan's and Linda's skates so they could tell them apart. Mom had to sweep the snow off the pond, and then we all went out on the pond. Skating was not an easy task. Mom loved it, so we went to the pond frequently to skate before spring came and melted the ice. Jan was always determined to do what she wanted, and so she learned to ice skate.

*   *   *

When Jan started kindergarten it was exciting for all of us. Linda and I wanted to go to school too, but fun as it would be, we had to wait. Jan still had her left eye sewn partially shut and was wearing thick glasses. She was no different than anyone else, except her left eye was partially closed. Jan was smart and could read better than I ever could. But Mrs. Swartz, her teacher, recommended that Mom and Dad let her do kindergarten over, because of her lack of balance and under-developed physical skills.

The next summer, we got a couple of old ink-well school desks and Jan, Linda, and I would line them up on the porch. Jan would be the teacher and teach Linda and me. We colored in coloring books, learned to count, and learned some of the ABC's. Jan, Linda, and I used to play together a lot since the neighbor kids were miles away from our farm home. We played house; we played doctor; we played army; and we played cowboys and Indians. We played in the barns. We were typical farm kids, enjoying life.

Jan and I started kindergarten together that fall. Jan was always resentful that she had to repeat kindergarten since she had gotten good grades. From kindergarten to the twelfth grade we were in the same grade and usually had the same teacher. At that time I didn't understand that others thought she was different. When we went to church, none of the kids treated her differently, maybe because we all grew up together. I don't know how Jan felt that year in kindergarten, but she probably wanted to know why people were mean, stared at her, or called her names. Or maybe she liked learning to read and write and didn't let it get to her.

In first grade I learned how cruel kids could be. We were on the playground, and this boy, Andy, was laughing and calling Jan names: "Blindie" and "Ugly". He said to her that she was as ugly as his butt. The teachers never did anything when other kids were bullying her or making fun of her. So I jumped onto that kid like a dog wanting to kill a calf. Luckily, I never got in trouble for that act. In those days if you got sent to the principal's office he could spank you if he thought it would facilitate your behavior and help you to be a better person.

*　　*　　*

Grandma Jones broke her ankle one spring, and it was in a cast. Linda and Jan loved to mimic people. One day, Grandma and Grandpa came over to visit. Jan and Linda were playing in the stairwell, and Jan had an oatmeal box on her leg and was pretending to be Grandma. Linda was playing Grandpa. In a whiny voice, Jan said, "Albert, help me." Grandma heard her and was shocked. She asked if she sounded like that. Everyone agreed that she did when she wanted Grandpa to do something for her. Grandpa was never called Albert by anyone except his mother and his wife and then only when Grandma wanted him to do something for her. He had been nicknamed Bill as a young boy.

In the 1960's, the hog market fell apart, putting a real hardship on Dad and Mom. Grandpa Jones, being a smart farmer, saw it coming and talked to Dad regarding selling his hogs before the prices plummeted.

Dad did sell the hogs and then bought Angus cattle and began to build a herd. We all had to lend a hand to help on the farm. I helped Mom with gardening and caring for the chickens. She was still working at Snowdon's. Jan loved to help Mom in the kitchen even though she would break things. Together they did the dishes, cleaned the floor, and cooked the meals. From the time Jan was three years old, she would climb up on the oven door to see what was cooking. One day Dad told Mom she should not let Jan climb on the oven door, as she might do it when the oven was hot. After thinking about it, Mom put a stop to it, and Grandpa made Jan a stool to stand on.

Mom had a set of twelve dishes given to her when she and Dad were married. With Jan helping in the kitchen that set became multiple parts of a set. My mother loved her children in spite of the difficulties. Mom gave those dishes, which are now a set of six, to her grandson, Josh, when he bought his house.

Jan, Linda, and I used to play on the tractor and pretend we could drive. One day when I was five, Dad taught me to drive the tractor. That summer, Blanche watched Jan and Linda so I could help Dad with the baled hay. He put me on the tractor, put it in first gear, and sent me down each row of hay while he loaded the low-boy. It was hard on him and took a lot of physical strength to load those bales.

One time, we three kids were playing in Dad's old Dodge car. Jan was in the driver's seat and one of us released the emergency brake. Dad came running after us as we headed down the hill on the old dirt road that separated the two barns and some property, yelling for us to steer into the barnyard gatepost. Jan did just what Dad said, and even though we missed the post, we came to a quick halt.

The summer nights were awesome as the family sat or laid under the stars. We caught lightening bugs, and Dad would name the planetary systems for us. Dad and Mom played with us, tossing us up in the air or swinging us by our arms, round and round. A lot of what Mom and Dad did would now be considered abusive. Back then, it was entertainment, especially since there was no TV except when we could con Mom into taking us to Grandma Jones's house or on Saturday night to the Coons.

One of our favorite past-times was listening to records on Dad and Mom's phonograph player. Jan like to sing and had taken baton lessons. She would twirl her baton around to the music and sing the songs she knew. Jan liked the Beatles, Simon and Garfunkel, Tony Orlando, and others, but Elvis Presley was her favorite.

*   *   *

One spring day Jan, Linda, and I were playing hide-and-seek. That seemed like a peaceful activity, but not this time. Jan was the seeker, and Linda and I were the hiders. I had found a double-edged razor in the trash and picked it out.

Jan said, "Ready or not, here I come!"

About that time I yelled out, "You better not find me, or I'll cut you!"

She came right to the sound of my voice. I cut her wrist, and she bled and bled. Linda and I were scared. Linda wanted to ring the dinner bell for Dad. I didn't because I knew what would happen, but we knew we had to ring that bell. This hundred-year old bell was left on the farm by my great grandfather. The bell was used to call the farmers out of the field at dinnertime. Mom used it to signal Dad when he was in the field: once meant "come," more than two rings meant "come running." It seemed like forever before Dad got there. Jan was bleeding, and I knew I had done something really bad.

I was right, Dad saw Jan's wrist was bleeding and put a tourniquet on her arm. Then he grabbed the butter paddle, and I don't believe I ever got a better, more well deserved whipping in my life. Off we went to Doc George's. I was scared; I thought Jan was going to bleed to death. Not only that, I thought Dad would continue where he left off on my rear with that butter paddle. To this day, double-edged razors give me the willies. I grew up and eventually moved my family to Colorado, and I now have that old bell in my yard in Colorado.

Jan was the kind of person who had to test everything. One day, she touched the old wood-burner stove that sat in the corner of our kitchen. Sometimes, Linda and I would dare her to touch it just for a laugh. She would touch it, and I know that it had to burn like hell. But her sensory perceptions were not normal, so she did not feel the burning. She was never burned deeper than a first-degree burn, and usually it was just red.

Jan would eat things that Linda and I wouldn't. Just as her eyes didn't tear, her mouth didn't seem to be able to taste and her nose was not capable of smelling much. Linda and I hated eggs. Dad would make us sit at the table until we ate all of our breakfast.

When we had eggs for breakfast, Linda would ask Dad, "If I eat my eggs can I leave the table?"

He would agree. She would eat her breakfast except the eggs. Then she would stuff her mouth full of eggs and go outside and spit them out. Luckily, most of the time our dog would be under the table, and our eggs got eaten by the dog.

CHAPTER 3

The Love of Animals

As farmers, my parents butchered their own beef and chickens. Mom canned fruits and vegetables. We had a lot of home-cooked variations to eat. It was all very healthy and cooked from scratch; very little came from cans or the store. Some of our evening meals were biscuits and gravy, cream of tuna on biscuits, cauliflower with cheese sauce, and during the winter, if we had a big meal at noon, we might just have popcorn or cornbread and milk for supper, but we always had plenty of good food to eat. One year as Dad butchered a steer Jan, Linda, and I watched. We sat there watching Dad pull the steer up to the rafter so he could skin it.

My sister Linda kept saying, "Poor cow." "Poor cow."

Linda would not eat any of the beef that year, but watching Mom behead a chicken so she could clean and cook it never seemed to bother Linda.

Dad would get pretty physical with Jan when he disciplined her. He said that she couldn't feel it if he didn't. One time, Uncle Cliff was visiting when Dad gave Jan a brutal whipping. Uncle Cliff told Dad that if he ever whipped Jan again he would give Dad a thrashing just like he did Jan. The whole thing caused a squabble between Dad and Mom. My father would sit in his room with his .22 Colt pistol on his lap, waiting for Uncle Cliff to show up. Cliff never showed, in fact he avoided my dad for years, as he was afraid Dad might shoot him. Since Jan's death, Dad has acknowledged that he never really knew what Jan was capable of doing, and he had not treated her fairly. He loves her memory and keeps a picture of her peeling potatoes at the kitchen sink on his refrigerator.

Grandpa Jones had told Dad and Mom that maybe they should make Dad's dog Sko stay out of the house. Grandpa thought that his shedding hair was causing Jan to have trouble with her eyes. Dad didn't agree, and Sko continued to live in the house with the rest of us. Mom didn't think it was a problem either. My dad loved Skochibit, which is Japanese for little one. He was a black, long-haired Irish setter mix. Even though Dad never liked nick names, he called his dog Sko. Sko was his buddy since before Dad moved to the farm, and he went everywhere with Dad. Dad like swimming in the pond on a hot humid day, and Iowa has plenty of those days. Sko went swimming in the pond with Dad and he went hunting with Dad.

We had some really ornery uncles. They drank and played pranks on whomever on any given day. They never meant any harm; they were just farm boys wanting to entertain themselves. My Uncle Cliff was by far the most malicious of all my uncles. He and Uncle Morris decided that if Dad wasn't going to keep Sko out of the house they would help. One day while Mom and Dad were in town, the boys took Sko out and shot him. Sko's shooting was a well-kept secret until I was forty years old, when Uncle Cliff told me the truth. The story seemed kind of funny to me because I know my uncles; I also thought it was unkind and cruel. I don't know if Dad ever knew what happened to Sko.

One time Uncle John and his wife, Darlene came by and brought with them a pup. We three were in love with that old pup and so was Dad. Dad said we should name him Bruno, and so now he had a name. He grew, and we all played with him, not knowing that, when there wasn't anyone around, he was chasing the calves and killing chickens. Once a dog gets a taste of blood, a farmer has to destroy the animal because they will always kill. One day, Dad came out with his .22 Colt pistol. We were swinging and playing with Bruno. Jan was riding an old tricycle that I had found at the dump one day with Grandpa Jones. Dad shot Bruno right there in front of us. My sisters and I didn't understand why. We were very angry with Dad. Dad told us about the calves, but it wasn't until later in life that I understood.

When we were about four, five, and six Dad and Mom got us a little Chihuahua. We named him Tinker. Jan loved to test everything, and got real good at getting Tinker to bite her. Linda and I would laugh and tell her to do it again, and she usually did.

Mom and Dad raised chickens. They had a white rooster that was the biggest rooster I ever saw. Jan would dare him to come after her, and he wouldn't budge. But I ran as hard as I could because he always came after me. I could be gathering firewood or getting a bucket of water from the well to take in the house, and sure enough there would be that old rooster. He would run and flog me, so run, I did.

My great-grandfather Samuel Parker Kane, had built our old farmhouse in 1906. It was a two-story, beautiful Victorian with a wrap around porch on two sides. It didn't have indoor plumbing except the small pump in the kitchen, which sat on the kitchen sink. This pump would freeze up every winter if it wasn't drained at night. We had an outhouse, which was near the house. In the wintertime, there was an old bucket in the pantry for Jan, Linda, and I to use.

Oh! What kids do! One pastime we liked, that I am sure Mom wasn't real pleased about, was dropping things in the cistern. This was a well near the house that the rain gutters drained into it from the roof of the house. It was not drinkable water, but it was piped into the small pump that sat on the sink in the kitchen. Mom used the water for laundry, dishes, cleaning, anything but drinking and cooking. We kids dropped a lot of Mom's silverware into the cistern just to hear them splash.

We had an old crank telephone that was on a party line. There was no such thing as a private line. Jan, Linda, and I use to like to listen when the phone rang. It was usually some-one we knew or thought we knew. We would laugh so the neighbors would hear us and they would say, "Is that you Jan? Or "Is that you Sam or Linda?" Then we would hang up, sometimes only to do it again. Oh the things we did while Mom and Dad were busy making a living.

*   *   *

Things always had to be Dad's Way. When he was a child, Dad always resented his parents insisting he let them know where he was, even though it might just be down the street to play with his buddies. One time, he was going to town and took me with him. He did not tell

Mom he was taking me. I guess he figured she would know. Dad was going to have the oil changed and some other work done on his car. He always took it to the same gas station, which was run by a distant relative of his. When Mom couldn't find me she called the neighbors to see if I was there, and I wasn't there. Mom called the gas station, and they had not seen Dad. Mom told them that I was missing, and she was worried. She said Dad was coming in for an oil change and would they please let him know that Sam was missing. When Dad got to the station and Charles saw me with him, he became very upset with Dad. He told Dad Mom was worried because I was missing and why had he not let her know he was taking me to town with him? Dad called Mom and told her I was with him. She was relieved but asked why he had not let her know. Dad never pulled that tactic again.

One summer Dad left home to go to Cripple Creek, Colorado, to work in the mines. Mom and her brothers baled the hay and did the farm work. Dad was gone a couple of months and then came home. He had decided he did not want to raise his family in a mining town. There were plenty of problems, since Dad had taken money out of the bank and left without telling Mom he was leaving or where he was going. When he came home it was late, and we had gone to bed. Mom always locked the door, and she heard a noise. When she realized someone had come through the pantry window, she reached down beside the bed and picked up the ball bat. All at once, the light over the desk in the dining room came on. This light was difficult to turn on if you didn't know how to do it. She knew it had to be Dad who had come through the window. She was very angry because he could have knocked on the bedroom window and woke her up. But no—Dad had to do it his way. As usual, Mom and Dad were able to work things out.

∗   ∗   ∗

We spent some time with our Jones Grandparents when Mom worked. Grandpa Jones loved his grandkids. Jan and Linda would sit one on each of his knees, playing with his pocket watch, tire pressure gauge, pencil, or pen. Our uncles loved us too and were good to us. They came to see us often, especially during our last days on the farm. Dad liked ice cream, and Grandma Jones would make a six-quart, hand-cranked freezer full of ice-cream mixture. The guys would crank it until it was solid ice cream. Dad liked to take the paddle and eat off it because it had a lot of ice cream on it.

He would say to Grandma, "Don't clean it all off."

One time, just for fun, Grandma lifted the paddle from the center of the freezer and handed it to Dad without removing any of the ice cream. He didn't say a word. It took him all afternoon, but he ate it all. Almost always someone showed up, uncles, aunts, great-uncles, great-aunts, great-grandparents, or cousins, to help eat the homemade ice cream.

I loved to catch salamanders and put them in our basement. One time, I was out with Grandpa Jones while he was putting up a fence. It had rained the night before, and I found a salamander in the post hole. I caught it, and when I took it to the house, Grandma made me turn it loose. She said it was poisonous. Saying something was poisonous was Grandma's way of getting rid of things she didn't like or didn't know anything about.

When people hear about our life on the farm in Iowa, they think there is no way we could have lived the way we did. Most of these people lived in cities and had no idea that in the 1960s there were still Americans without electricity, running water, and growing their own food.

We were a good Seventh Day Adventist Christian family. We went to church every Sabbath. We ate all our meals at the table; Dad always said grace before we ate. But without a doubt, while eating at the table Jan would spill something, and Dad either yelled at her to be more careful or he would slap her. He never connected her poor vision to her clumsiness.

We were brought up in the old tradition where children were to be seen and not heard. Maybe this was why Jan wasn't open to anyone. Our paternal grandparents were guilty of following this old motto, especially if there were adult guests around. Mom did not support this theory, as she did not want her children to grow up shy and bashful. She loved her children and we were well behaved and polite when company came.

CHAPTER 4

Mom's Dream Comes True

Mom was working at Snowdons, but she felt a strong desire to go to nursing school. She did not tell Dad of her ambition. She wanted to be accepted in a school before she broke the news to him. She applied at several schools in Des Moines and schools near by, but no one would take a married student.

Mom and Dad had been taking Bible studies when Mom got the flu. Dad was studying with her as she lay in bed. Mom felt this urge to tell Dad what she felt but she knew he was going to say, "We can't afford it; it's out of the question." Mom prayed about it. Dad realized something was on Mom's mind and asked her what was bothering her. She told him that she felt led by the Lord to become a nurse.

He said, "There is no way. We can't afford it." And with the next breathe he said, "But if you really feel this is what the Lord wants, we will do it."

They talked about it and agreed they would sell the farm so Mom could go to nursing school. Dad told Mom to apply to some schools, but he did not want to go west of the Mississippi River.

One week at church, one of the junior class members left their *Junior Guide* magazine in a pew. Mom picked it up, and in it several schools of nursing were listed. Most of them were west of the Mississippi River.

Mom considered Union College, a school in Lincoln, Nebraska, but after two years there, she would have to go to Boulder, Colorado, for two years. She did not think that was a good idea since Dad might not be able to find a job in both of those areas.

She wrote several schools but most of them did not take married students or they had the class already filled. Paradise Valley School of Nursing in National City, California, near San Diego, was a three-year diploma school established in 1909. Mom applied and was told she would have to take a chemistry class before she could be accepted. Mom enrolled at Drake University in Des Moines, the summer of 1963. She notified Paradise Valley School of Nursing that she was taking a six week chemistry class at Drake University.

Mom completed the chemistry class with a B and sent her GPA to Paradise Valley School of Nursing. They sent her a notice saying that since she had not been corresponding with them, they had filled the class.

A friend that Mom had grown up with was a doctor at Loma Linda University in Loma Linda, California and was home on vacation. He told Mom to write Paradise Valley School of Nursing again and tell them that she was on the way to California. If they still did not accept her, then she should get a job and apply at Loma Linda University for the following year.

*   *   *

Our Grandparents took care of us kids while Mom went to Drake University. My sister Linda was a bit of a tease and would do something to annoy me and I would retaliate by saying "Niña Stop that."

I would sometimes hit her, and then I would get in trouble. Then one day, Nonnie started observing what was going on. Jan and I were sitting in the floor playing a game. Linda walked by and gently stepped on my fingers, just enough to annoy me. Nonnie saw her and told us the story about the little boy who cried wolf one time to many. I think Linda got the message. After that Linda would join us playing instead of aggravating me. And I never got into trouble anymore.

*   *   *

In August 1963, we were packed and ready to go. San Diego here we come. Dad stayed behind until the loan of the people who were buying the farm went through. Dad sold the cattle, a couple of lambs Grandpa Jones had given me, and other livestock at the sale barn in Osceola. My bantam chicks, the other chickens, the furniture, and farm machinery were auctioned off at the farm.

To anyone who saw our 1959 Black Rambler, we must have really looked like the Beverly Hillbillies. That old Rambler was packed full. The top of the car carried a chest of drawers packed with dishes and clothes; the trunk was so full it had to be tied shut. If we had a flat tire Mom, would have had to unload the trunk to get to the spare. The back-seat was packed from top to floor and side-to-side but there was room for one of us kids to ride in the back. The other two rode up front with Mom. By the time we got to Kansas, we had the back-seat burrowed out so the two girls could sit in the back and play with their Barbie dolls.

Grandpa Kane had laid out our trip to Phoenix, Arizona, and then Uncle Cecil mapped the rest of the way for us. The hardest thing in our lives was saying good-bye to Dad that day and watching out the window as the old white house and the red barns disappeared.

Us kids had never been out of the state of Iowa, except once. Mom's brother Don had died at age twenty-six from a leaky heart valve. He was married with a one-year-old daughter and a son on the way. We stayed with Nonnie and Grandpa Kane while Mom and Dad went to Don's funeral in Minnesota. Later, we went with Grandpa and Grandma Jones to Minnesota to help our Aunt Dorothy, Don's wife, for a short time.

So the idea of California, the ocean, and the big city had a lot of excitement to it. I know Mom had to have been scared out of her mind. Mom had never driven on a long trip without another adult being with her and had never been beyond the states connecting to Iowa. And now all she knew was we were on our way to National City, California and to the Paradise Valley School of Nursing. We had nowhere to stay when we arrived. Mom had three loud and noisy kids in the car. The little Chihuahua Tinker stayed behind to be a companion for Dad. Whenever we reached a large city, Mom would tell us to be quiet so she wouldn't get lost. When we saw a city limit sign, we obliged her, reminding each other to be quiet even though the town might only have a population of one-hundred people.

We left Iowa and headed south to Kansas City, Missouri, and then across Kansas. What a boring drive it was across the flat land of Kansas. We would count the cars from states other than the state we were in and kept track of the numbers to see who saw the most out of state cars. We went through Colorado Springs and thought it was so beautiful. Mom told us that at one time Dad wanted to attend the Colorado School of Mines and get his degree in geology, but he never did. We then went on to Albuquerque, New Mexico, where our car got drowned out trying to cross a dip in the highway that was flooded. A nice gentleman with a big pickup pulled us through, and we got on our way. We did a lot of sight-seeing on that trip, even though we didn't do a lot of stopping.

We drove to the Petrified Forest National Park in Arizona and stopped for a break. Mom didn't like the thought of driving over the mountains. She thought the further south we went, the lower the mountains would be, so instead of driving to Flagstaff we headed south through Fort Apache. Little did she know that those mountains were worse, since it was a two-lane highway and very crooked. You could look down and see where you were going to be, and then going up on the other side of the mountain, you could look back and see where you had been. By this time, we kids were ready to call it enough. One of us and sometimes all three of us would ask Mom when we were going to reach Uncle Cec's house.

Mom would reply, mile after mile, "Tomorrow I hope."

*   *   *

When we reached the southeast suburban town of Chandler, near Phoenix, Mom stopped and called Uncle Cecil. There were no cell phones then, and Cecil lived on the North side of Phoenix. Uncle Cecil wasn't home from work and Aunt Vera talked with Mom. Vera was worried because Mom had not followed the directions given to her to get to Phoenix and she just knew Mom would get lost. Mom took the directions that had been given to her before we left Iowa and reversed them using a map for assistance, and we arrived at Uncle Cec's around 5:00 p.m. Cec was home and had been waiting for our call so he could come and get us. He couldn't understand why we took the long way around, even though Mom told him why.

When we arrived, Uncle Cec gave mom a letter from Dad. It contained a letter from Paradise Valley School of Nursing. Someone had dropped out and they were accepting Mom into the program. That was one burden lifted off Mom. Wow, was she happy to get this letter from Dad. Now she was really certain this was the work of the Lord.

Cecil and Vera had a son, Larry and two daughters, Jo and Beverly. They were all older than us; in fact, Jo was about Mom's age. Larry had scarlet fever at age seven and his fever got so high it caused him to have brain damage. His IQ was never more than third graders. Larry was about sixteen years older than me. As young kids, my sisters and I didn't realize that he was different. I don't think we even cared, because he knew how to play lots of games and we liked games. He didn't say anything about Jan being different.

Cecil and Vera had a color TV, and we had never seen one. We never even had a black and white TV in Iowa. We met Cec and Vera's daughters, Dad's cousins. Jo was married to Larry, an Air Force man. He was stationed at Luke Air Force Base, Arizona, in the Special Forces and flew rescue helicopters. He had been shot in Vietnam and was sent home with a serious wound. I believe that was the first time I had ever heard about the Vietnam War or knew anyone associated with it. Beverly was dating an Air Force pilot and later married him.

Our visit with Uncle Cec and Aunt Vera had come to an end. Cec loaded us up with some oranges off his trees and pointed us in the right direction.

*   *   *

At that time, what has become Interstate 8 was Highway 80, a two-lane road all the way to San Diego, California. Those last miles took forever. It was miles and miles of desert that was fascinating to us Iowa kids but boring at the same time. Then came some crooked mountain roads. My sisters and I slept a lot during that hot, dirty drive, with no air conditioner and all four windows rolled down. Once in a while we would sing, but mostly we were just loud and noisy.

It was early August when we finally arrived in San Diego with its miles and miles of city. It was a small city then compared to what it is today, but to a bunch of farmers it was totally unique, spell bounding, and unreal. There were cars, lots of cars and people and houses, and tall buildings. I remember the tallest building was the old Grant Hotel with Mr. A's Restaurant on top. Years later, I learned Mr. A's had a 360 degree view of San Diego.

We drove to the end of Highway 80 and Mom stopped at a gas station to ask how to get to National City. The attendant told her to go south on Highway 101, and it would take her to National City. When we arrived in National City we drove around to see Paradise Valley Hospital and Sanitarium and the school where we would be going. It was getting late, so we found a motel and ate at Oscar's Restaurant. This became our restaurant of choice. There never will be a better burger.

The next day Mom drove around looking for an apartment where we could live. Mom talked to landlord after landlord, but no one wanted to rent to a woman with three kids even though our Dad was coming later. We stopped at one apartment complex, and the landlady told her they didn't rent to people with children. Mom had been praying about this, and when she heard this her face fell and she looked so sad and discouraged.

She explained to the lady how we got there, and that she going to be attending Paradise Valley School of Nursing.

The landlady said to my mom, "You know, we have a duplex a few blocks from the hospital and the renters are moving out. You can rent this duplex, but you will have to wait until they are out and we inspect it."

Mom told her not to worry about cleaning it, as she would do that. It was a two-bedroom duplex with a detached garage. Mom then asked if she could unload her car into the garage. The lady told Mom she would have to talk to the current tenants. When we drove to the duplex, we learned that the renters were moving to the Los Angeles area to work in White Memorial Hospital. He had been the head of the laboratory at Paradise Valley Hospital. They were moving out the next day. He helped unloaded our car into the garage and we went back to the motel.

The next day, we went furniture shopping. That was an endless nightmare for Mom. We finally settled in with just enough used furniture to do until Dad arrived.

The weekend arrived, and we went to church at the Paradise Valley Church. When Jan, Linda, and I walked into the Seventh Day Adventist church that first Sabbath it was a day like none other. We were use to a small-town church with maybe six kids in the class. But this Sabbath school class had at least thirty kids. We were all kindergarteners, except

Jan. Because she was older, she went next door. I'm sure it was hard on her with all the kids looking at her and probably making fun of her looks. Jan, Linda, and I had never been separated, and it was hard to accept. We also were used to a very small church of twenty-five to thirty members. This church had a membership of 1200.

CHAPTER 5

Beginning A New Life

It was hot and dry in California, much better than the hot, humid summer weather of Iowa. The beach was the first place we went after moving into our new home. The beach became an addiction for Jan, Linda, and I all through our lives. We loved to cross over the bay to Coronado Island on the ferry. If you were on the bay and it was foggy, you could hear the tugboats go through the fog taking the Navy ships in and out of the harbor. We spent many a Sabbath afternoon at the zoo or the Museum of Natural History in Balboa Park, which was one of Dad's favorite places to visit.

The last week of August arrived, and it was time to start school. The first day of school we were all anxious, including Mom. Mom took us to school and then went to the dormitory classrooms to start her nurse's training. This meant we needed someone to watch us when Mom had evening classes and until she came home after her day of school. People were friendly and most of our neighbors were more than happy to help look after us.

Mom had become friends with our neighbors who lived across the double driveway of our duplexes. Betty would watch us when Mom had evening classes. One day, Betty's boys got her matches. Her boys, Jan, and Linda were lighting the matches. Betty thought it was Linda and

Jan's fault that they had gotten her matches and was playing with them, so she burnt Jan and Linda with a cigarette to teach them a lesson. Linda still has a scar from where Betty had put the lighted end of the cigarette between her fingers and held it.

Mom had also made friends with Gay and Joe who lived in the front duplex across the driveway. Joe was in the Navy and was shipped out to sea every six months. Mom did not have classes on Friday, and since Gay did not drive, Mom would take her to the commissary. They would go out to lunch, and then shopping. After Betty burned Jan's arm and Linda's fingers, Gay started watching us.

*   *   *

Jan was in the second grade, as was I, and Linda was in first grade. Janet, a neighbor girl, walked to and from school with us. It was hard to keep up with her as she was tall and older and walked fast so we wouldn't be late. She would hold Jan's hand to help her up the steps on the steep wooded hill behind the hospital. It seemed like such a long walk. We weaved through the buses and on to our classrooms at the far eastern corner of the school, right beside the playground. Jan hadn't made friends as fast as Linda and I. I always saw Jan out of the corner of my eye. I saw the kids that didn't treat her right, and I saw her make friends. Her first friend was Marla. Then Jan made friends with Violet and Nancy. When Jan made friends they saw her and accepted her for who she was, not how she looked.

She did not have a lot of friends, but she was a person who didn't need a lot of friends to be happy.

It was hard for Jan going to a new school, which was a private Seventh Day Adventist Academy. This made a vital change in Jan for the rest of her life. All of us were going to start our new life without knowing what the future would hold.

I started to avoid Jan when we arrived in California and started to school. I loved and protected her, but I guess I became ashamed of the way she looked and her clumsiness. I afterward told her how sorry I was for the wrongs I did to her. These emotions of mine lasted pretty much the rest of Jan's life. Jan was a forgiving person, and Mom has assured me Jan had forgiven me long before I forgave myself and that Jan thought of me as her "loving, protective brother".

Mom started getting calls almost every day from the school, because Jan was crying and they could not figure out why. Mom would go get her and take her home, but Jan never told her what the problem was. It was making it difficult for Mom to go to nursing school when she had to take time out to go get Jan. Everyone thought it was because of a new school, kids making fun of her looks, and having to make new friends. Maybe Jan thought it would be easy to make friends going to a Christian school. But the majority of kids are the same everywhere.

*   *   *

The farm had been sold with the machinery, furniture, and animals and Dad was on his way. He stopped along the way for gas, and as he got out Tinker, the Chihuahua, tried to jump out and Dad not knowing slammed the car door on Tinker. Dad thought he was dead. As he drove on through the desert he was going to bury Tinker, but in doing so he noticed Tinker move. He put him back in the car, fed and watered him, and came on to California. Dad arrived in November just before Thanksgiving. Being away from Dad had been a lonely time for all of us, especially Mom. Linda and I would talk about how we missed Dad, but Jan never said a word. When Jan heard his car pull up, she dashed out the door, jumped into his arms, and that was the end of Mom getting calls from school. Jan had missed Dad, but never let anyone know.

Dad began looking for a job but there was none to be found. Just when he was about to give up finding a job, the hospital called him to come work in the food service. He worked from 11:00 am to 7:00 pm. He ordered supplies and kept the shelves stocked, and in the evening he would supervise the Academy high-school boys who worked in the hospital kitchen doing dishes, cleaning the floors, etc. Dad's work always had a Halloween party and a Christmas party with a Santa Clause. The kids always received a gift, and we always looked forward to Dad's yearly parties.

Jan was always rather quiet, never letting go of her true feelings or emotions. Linda and I almost always were the authority during play. Jan never really told anyone about anything that was bothering her. I thought Mom would become the director of what Jan would do. But Mom only encouraged and reassured her rather than pressure her into doing things that she knew Jan wanted to do or should do. Jan was determined and strong willed but needed Mom's reassurance. Jan in effect was a supporter. She never had more than two or three friends at a time in school or even in the neighborhood.

Jan loved playing on the parallel bars, the swing, and the monkey bars. The teachers did not want her to play on the bars. Because of her vision, they were afraid she might fall and hurt herself. She asked her second-grade teacher when she could play on them. The teacher told her maybe when she was nine years old. Little did the teacher realize she would soon be nine. Jan, Linda, and Jan's friend Rhonda went back after school on Jan's ninth birthday. Jan crossed the parallel bars, and as she got to the end, she missed the last bar and fell breaking her left arm. She went home, showed her arm to Dad and told him what she had done. Both bones in her forearm near her wrist were displaced, so Dad knew they were broken. He took her to see Dr. Maloney, who sent her to the hospital so her arm could be x-rayed and put in a cast. Jan was left-handed, so what a time she had trying to write. Jan's pain threshold was zilch, so she never complained of pain. She would burn herself or cut herself but never a tear, because she felt little or no pain and had a small amount of tears.

Mom's nursing class was an active class. They would have weekend outings at the Descanso Lodge, which was in the Laguna Mountains and owned by the hospital. The female students stayed in one dorm and the guys in another. When the spouse of a married student or teacher attended the weekend outing, they had their own cabins. They made taffy and had taffy pulls. We hiked, and played all kinds of games. Jan was hiking with Charlotte, a nursing student, and was beginning to whine as she was traveling up the mountain. Charlotte told her to swing her arms to help her momentum and so she could have better balance and walk easier. After that, Jan loved to hike.

On our first Christmas in California, Linda, Jan, and I wanted bikes. Mom and Dad were afraid Jan would get hit by a car or fall and injure herself because of her balance and clumsiness, so they never bought her a bike. That spring Mom came home from class and found Jan riding Linda's bike on the street in our court. She asked her who taught her to ride the bike.

Jan said, "Oh, I been borrowing Linda's bike and learned to ride it by myself."

Mom asked her if Linda knew she had been riding her bike, and Jan said "No."

The next Christmas, the girls wanted roller skates. Dad didn't think Jan should have skates, as she could get hurt on them. Mom reminded him we used to ice skate, and since Jan had mastered the bike she felt Jan would be careful on roller skates. So Mom bought the girls skates for Christmas. Jan did not take them off Christmas Day until late afternoon, when she could finally stand up on them. When Jan wanted something after that there was never any question or hesitation about her getting it.

*   *   *

Before Mom graduated from nursing school, we moved into a two-bedroom house on the hospital grounds. It was an old Victorian, two bedroom, single-story house. The garage had been converted to an extra room and the laundry room. That room became my bedroom, and the girls had bunk beds in a bedroom in the house. This house was larger and closer to the hospital and to our school than the duplex had been.

Mom's parents believed everything had its place and everything belonged in its place. Dad was so organized he wanted his shirts facing the same way in the closet. I guess I learned from Mom and Dad to be organized. I had a collection of things I made: boats, airplanes, and the like. One day, Mom cleaned my room and moved some of my things. I was not happy with her; after all, everything belongs in its place.

I could never stand to see someone hurting or picking on another person or an animal, probably because of what they did to Jan. One day, we were sitting in the dining room eating when I looked out the window and saw the neighbor boy who was a few years older than me, throw a cat up in the air and let it fall to the ground. I got up from the table and dashed out the door. My parents did not know what was going on and they followed me to the door but by this time I had lowered this boy to the ground.

We made new friends after moving. Jan became friends with Rhonda and Denise, and I became friends with Denise's brother, Damian. Jan, Linda, and Violet played together, and I became friends with Violet's brother, Kenny. Their parents worked at the hospital, and they lived on hospital grounds except for Rhonda, who lived just around the corner from us. It seemed as though we boys played a lot of warfare games. Wrestling was a favorite. I was pretty good, and Damian would bring dudes from his school to try and stop me. I don't ever remember getting beat, probably because if Damian or I were losing the other bounded in to help out. The girls mostly played house, jumped rope, roller skated, or sang and danced to Motown music.

∗   ∗   ∗

The 1960s were the beginning of "Revolutionary Rights." In 1963, Martin Luther King, a Baptist minister, lead the Civil Rights movement. His famous speech was "I have a dream." In 1966, Equal Rights Marches began in an effort to end segregation and racial discrimination. Riots broke out in Los Angeles and San Diego. Our friends, the Combs, attended a black church and were coming home from church one Sabbath when a brick was thrown into their windshield. Eventually, all became normal again. April 1968 Martin Luther King gave his last important speech in a Mason Temple church in Georgia. It was called "I have been to the Mountain Top." He was assassinated August 1968, and Malcolm X tried to take the movement into other areas.

On November 22, 1963, President John F. Kennedy was killed by an assassin's bullet as his motorcade drove through Dallas, Texas. I was in second grade, and we were at lunch when we learned that President Kennedy had been shot. I will never forget that day; so much grief. I don't think America ever completely got over his death. Kennedy's memorable edict was "Ask not what your country can do for you—ask what you can do for your country." Before his death, he laid plans for a massive attack on the endless vessels of hardship and poverty.

Robert 'Bobby" Kennedy, President John F Kennedy's brother, was US Attorney General. He pursued a relentless crusade against organized crime and the Mafia. Robert Kennedy was persistent in his pursuit of the Teamsters President, Jimmy Hoffa, because of Hoffa's corruption in financial and electoral matters. Kennedy was committed to civil rights enforcement. On June 5, 1968, after winning the California primary, Robert Kennedy left the ballroom to greet supporters working in the hotel's kitchen. In the kitchen passageway, Sirhan Sirhan, a twenty-four year-old Palestinian, opened fire with a .22 caliber revolver and shot

Kennedy in the head at close range. Kennedy died the next day in The Good Samaritan Hospital.

All these killings really had an effect on us kids, even though we were only ten to twelve years old. It seemed as though this nation was filled with cruel, ruthless, uncaring, unfeeling, merciless, hardhearted, brutal people. Has it really changed? Those years made such an impact on me that I can never forget.

CHAPTER 6

New Adventures

Even though we were on a tight budget, Mom and Dad always seemed to put a roof over our head and food on the table. Even as a student, Mom worked some evenings and weekends. The hospital would call to see if Mom could work. Mom apparently had a young-sounding voice.

Linda would answer the phone and they would ask, "Can you work today?"

Linda would say, "I can't but my mom might. Let me get her."

Those were also the years when there was a nursing shortage, and the government gave nursing students loans. If a student worked five years after they became a registered nurse they only had to pay back a small percentage of the loan. Mom was one of those lucky students; she not only worked five years but worked forty-five or more years.

In 1965, the Paradise School of Nursing wanted to build a swimming pool. They sold candy to raise the money and eventually raised enough with donations to accomplish their wish. I helped sell candy for the swimming pool project. I sold more candy than any of the nursing students. Mom asked me how I could sell so much candy.

"Well it is easy," I told her, "When I knock on a door and the lady is overweight I always go back because I know she will buy something."

We thought the pool was great as it meant a lot of pool time for us kids. If we weren't in the school pool, then Mom and Dad would take us to the beach. Jan loved the water. I could never figure out how she managed to swim in the riptide at the beach, when her eyesight was so bad.

Mom graduated from nursing in June 1966. She had reached her dream and God's will. Dad and Mom made many sacrifices, as did all of us, but it paid off.

In 1968, the Paradise Valley School of Nursing closed. It was a three-year diploma school and the two-year AA degree at White Memorial Hospital in Los Angeles had come into effect. Most students thought if they went two years and got an associate degree they would be better off, so Paradise Valley School of Nursing had to close its doors due to lack of students.

Grandma and Grandpa Jones could not get away for Mom's graduation and came later. Nonnie and Grandpa came from Iowa for Mom's graduation. We had a wonderful time with Nonnie and Grandpa while they were there and did a lot of things with them. We went to Sea World and Jan leaned over the edge of the dolphin pool and her glasses slid off her face. The girl who was training with that particular dolphin dived in and rescued Jan's glasses. Jan was so happy and thankful to have her glasses back.

Nonnie and Grandpa had planned to stay ten days, but after about a week, Jan was yelling at Mom and giving her a hard time about everything and nothing. One day, Jan was mean and yelling at Mom. Mom could not get her to settle down so she took her in the bedroom and paddled her with a ping-pong paddle.

Grandpa told Nonnie, "I think we have worn our welcome out" and they left the next day.

Jan did not want them to leave, but they felt she was jealous because they were getting Mom's time and she wanted her attention.

Before leaving Iowa, I had heard about California's earthquakes. After moving to California when I would hear a booming sound, I would run for the house as I thought it was an earthquake. Mom did not know what I was afraid of. One day, she was outside with me, and I heard the boom and told Mom we had better get in the house as there was an earthquake coming. She realized it was the sonic boom of a plane going through the sound barrier. She told me what I was hearing and reassured me we were safe. Then, in 1967, we did have an earthquake. Mom was working in the operating room and the X-ray machines were swinging back and forth on their tracks. Mom was concerned about us kids and called home. Jan and Linda were at home and Jan told Mom the water in the toilet splashed out of the commode but they were okay. Mom asked Jan where I was. Our friends, Gay and Joe, had bought a house a few miles from us. Jan told Mom I was at their house playing with their son Joey. Mom called Gay to see if I was scared. Gay told Mom that Joey and I were out on the bank playing with our cars and did not even know there had been an earthquake. We had wondered why our cars were moving on their own. I never felt the earth move, but according to Gay it had.

*   *   *

My Uncle Gene and his wife Joanne moved to California. They lived in a hospital house and both of them worked at the hospital. Gene worked in central supply and Joanne worked in the physical therapy department. We loved Gene and Joanne and spent a lot of time at their house, especially since it was across from the swimming pool. We needed an adult to swim with us, and Uncle Gene was easy to con into doing things. When the school of nursing closed in 1968, the hospital took over the pool and had a lifeguard, which meant paying twenty-five cents to swim. Later, after the school closed, the dormitory was torn down, and the pool was filled in for a parking lot.

One summer, Gene and Joann took Jan, Linda, and I on a vacation to Iowa with them. Gene had a big, old, 1958 Pontiac. The old Pontiac broke down getting there, and Gene hadn't budgeted for extras. He managed to repair the car, and we eventually arrived in Osceola, Iowa. We loved visiting our Kane and Jones Grandparents. Jan and Linda loved to play house, and that summer Uncle John's car was their pretend car. There was only one problem: the garden hose became the gas station and water was pretend gas, which doesn't make a car run. All my uncles loved us kids, and thank God, because anyone else would have been really angry. But Uncle John just laughed and told Jan and Linda that it was an easy fix.

That summer at age twelve was the first time I had ever smoked or drank. Gene, Tom, David and a cousin took me fishing, and I caught a fish in East Lake. I thought I should give smoking and drinking a try. I did, but I didn't like it.

Gene and Dave kept saying "Murray would kill us if he knew."

I thought it made me cool like my uncles and Kane grandparents so eventually I took up the evil habits.

Summer was over, and it was time to return to San Diego. The old Pontiac quit on us again. This time in the hottest place in the United States: Needles, California. Gene was out of money and he needed an alternator and fuel to finish the trip. It was hot; we were hungry and thirsty with no money. He had to call Mom for help. She wired him money to get his car fixed and to buy us some food. While we were waiting on the money to arrive, I got so hot that I became sick. The rest area had water but it wasn't healthy to drink. An older couple stopped. It's not often someone will stop in 120 degree heat, but they did. They gave us some crackers and water. It wasn't much but better than nothing. Gene and Joanne let Jan, Linda, and I eat while they did without. They told us that they had spare tires (they meant they were overweight) and could wait. When we were in Iowa, we had butchered a goat and lamb and had them frozen in the ice chest, but by the time we decided we were really hungry, they had thawed out and spoiled. Eventually we were on the road again. We stopped for a long-needed meal and some cold water before heading home.

∗   ∗   ∗

Finally, we arrived home. In the drive way was a brand-new, beautiful, blue, 1967 Dodge Dart. That wasn't the only surprise. Dad and Mom had bought a new house in Chula Vista, California. We knew they had been considering a house, because we had spent time looking at homes. Eventually, we got a TV and a console turntable with AM/FM radio. In our family that was like history being made. Of course, Dad took control of the TV when he was home. If he didn't want to watch a show, off went the TV. Thank goodness he wasn't always home. Jan loved game shows, like "The Dating Game," "The Newlyweds," and "You Bet Your Life." Linda liked soaps, and I liked westerns. Jan pretty much lived for "I Love Lucy" and we all watched "Bewitched."

Dad was interested in geology and rocks, so we would go camping in the desert one weekend a month from March through October.

Sometimes we would go to Julian to pan gold or to Pala to look for tourmaline crystals. Jan loved camping, but the hot, dry, dusty climate was too much for Jan's eyes and she had to use eye drops continuously.

Uncle Gene decided to go to college and get a nursing degree. He went to school three semesters and then quit. He and Joanne began having problems and, eventually, were divorced. Joanne went back to Iowa. Gene stayed in California and lived with us. He got a job at the University of California San Diego in the mental-health department, but he returned to Iowa after a few years.

*   *   *

I will never forget that first day in the sixth grade in Valley Lindo, our new school in Chula Vista. Linda and I didn't like the change. Jan however, didn't seem to have butterflies like we did, at least you never knew it. The sixth grade was most likely the grade when I really learned. This was the first time I was in a single class, and Jan was in a loft, a fifth and sixth mix. I think the public school system stereotyped Jan for the first time in her life. They put me in a higher-learning class and Jan in a lower class when it should have been the other way around. The school told Mom and Dad that maybe she should be in a special ed class. Mom wouldn't have it. Special classes would mean she wasn't up to par, and it would hold her back from ever being equal to the other students. She would have had to ride a little, orange van to and from a special school. Maybe those who rode it and were classified as disadvantaged would have had a better life if they hadn't been stereotyped. I knew some of these kids and never did know what problems they had. How sad it was to separate a child from the so-called norm because of ADHD, blindness, or a wheelchair.

Jan was not in a special school because her ophthalmologist did not tell Mom that Jan was legally blind until Jan was eighteen years old. Mom asked him why he had not told them. He said he knew Dad would have wanted to put her in a special school. The ophthalmologist had a handicapped child and had put her into a special school. He said it was the worst thing he ever did for her.

Linda and I made friends right away. Jan eventually made friends with a neighbor girl, Brenda, and her sister, Debbie. My first friend at Valley Lindo was a neighbor kid, Charlie Evans. His dad was in the

Navy and they had always lived in Navy housing, so Charlie's ways took time to get use to. Linda made friends with Andrea and Robin.

Whenever Jan was being harassed or called names, I'd get even one way or another. There was a Mexican-American boy playing on the parallel bars making fun of Jan. I helped him to the ground with no trouble. Another kid use to circle around Jan, saying all kinds of nasty, hateful, malicious things to her. I had my fill of him, and one day I stopped him in his tracks. It hurt me to see them bully my sister. I know now that the biggest problem with these kids was curiosity, and they just didn't understand. Apparently, not much respect and discipline was taught at home. A lot of the kids at Valley Lindo were Navy kids and their dads were at sea or in Vietnam.

The neighborhood we lived in was white. A black family bought a house down the street. Some of the neighbors tried to buy them out, but lost in court. Later, some of our neighbors moved. It seemed like a way for adults to bully someone. In the '60's there was a lot of discrimination, and the disadvantaged were treated as such. It wasn't until 1995 that the Disabled Discrimination Act went into effect and gave these people equal rights, wheel chair ramps, and doors wide enough to accommodate wheelchairs and other rights.

Aunt Gay and Joe gave Jan a Pekinese dog. Jan named him Ching-a-Ling. Jan loved that longhaired, flat-faced dog. Ching-a-Ling was blind in one eye, and Jan might have felt there was a common bond. Of course being a good brother I wasn't very nice to Ching-a-ling. I don't know why, but I just could not seem to keep from aggravating him. Ching-a-Ling developed severe arthritis and had problems getting around. Dad used a silencer and shot him in our garage. We buried him in the back yard under the palm tree.

During the days at school, I never showed Jan any friendship or acknowledged to anyone or to her that I was her brother, but everyone knew in spite of my cover-up. In the sixth grade, I began to have an interest in girls. I felt like they wouldn't give me the time of day because of my sister Jan and how she looked, but I was wrong. I never had a problem with girls other than me being a bit too shy.

Halloween on our block was an exciting time. We dressed up in costumes, and no one knew who was who nor did they care. Some would slit other kid's candy sacks so the candy would fall out and then picked it up for themselves. Jan and some of her friends were easy pickings. Some-how, they knew I was part of these pickpockets.

Christmas was Jan's favorite holiday, maybe because it was a time of peace. She actually loved all holidays, Easter, the Fourth of July and, parades with all the floats and fire-works. I am not sure how well she could see the floats and fireworks or how they appeared to her, but it gave her a feeling of contentment and she loved it. Even after she grew up, she decorated the house for all the holidays. I think all of this gave her sense of peace in a world that was cruel to her.

Jan was starting to do a lot of cooking. Mom would help her or sometimes read the recipe for her. Jan could read the recipes if she held them close to her face. She loved to make apple spice cake or any kind of upside-down cake. She was good at cooking and kept getting better and better until she was doing all the cooking, doing dishes, and cleaning the kitchen. She was a built-in chef and cleaning lady for Mom.

We were at an age when we wanted an allowance, but had to work for it. Linda was assigned cleaning the bathroom and vacuuming. My job was the yard work. I mowed the grass, and Mom would help with weeding the flowers. I swept the patio and cleaned up the weeds. Dad didn't do much except go to work. He always said work around the house and yard was what kids were for, although I doubt he ever did any work as a kid.

School was winding down, and we had our graduation parties going from sixth grade to junior high (now called middle school). On the last day of school, two sisters from Jan's class and a brother from my class had a dance at their home. It was chaperoned by their parents. There was dancing and snack food. This was a first-time thing for Jan and me. At school that week everyone was trying to pair up for the dance. Jan had a great time dancing with all her friends and listening or singing to the music. I enjoyed the party too, but was a little bit shy about dancing with the girls.

Jan would take bus trips to visit Grandpa and Grandma Jones in Iowa and Grandpa and Nonnie in Arizona. She and Mom also made trips to Iowa and Arizona and later to Colorado when we had moved there. Jan kept a log of every trip she took.

Mom and we kids went to Iowa to see family, when we came home, Dad had bought a piano. Jan and Linda both had wanted to take piano lessons since Nonnie was a pianist and taught piano. The teacher they had was an opera singer, and when she found out Jan liked to sing, she spent a lot of time with Jan's music. Jan enjoyed singing right up to the day she died. Her piano teacher taught her to sing as well as to play the piano. Jan would do solos in church, and everyone loved her music.

She stopped singing and dropped piano after hearing Dad say to Mom, "Handicapped people do not belong in front of an audience."

When Jan would go visit Nonnie and Grandpa Kane she would sing while Nonnie played the piano and sometimes she would play the piano. Nonnie and Grandpa both enjoyed her musical talent. Linda did not like the teacher and became involved in other things and, then quit piano.

Dad and Mom had a swimming pool built in our back-yard. We thought that was going to be the greatest summer ever. Only thing was, it all went away when the pool company took all summer to build our pool. Once it was finished, we would swim in the pool from early spring to late fall every year. The pool was close to the back of the house. Mom started working the 11:00pm-7:00am shift so she could be at home with us. She would come home and go to bed, trusting us kids to be safe. It was not until we were grown that she found out my friends and I use to jump off the roof of her bedroom into the pool.

CHAPTER 7

No Child Should Be Left Behind

Seventh grade was hard on Jan. Not only did the guys treat her like she was a dog but so did a lot of the girls. In her gym class a girl named Heather was about as cruel as a little bitch could be. I decided I was going to get even with her. My Dad had bought me a Honda 90 motorcycle, and she just happened to get in my way. I didn't see her just her piled up scooter. Luckily, she did not get hurt.

One dude wanted to fight me on a daily basis. I kept avoiding him. He would call Jan names, ask if she was retarded, and how come she's so ugly, and I couldn't take it anymore.

We were going to have a football game and guess what I was going to win over this dude. Football is a good way to fight without anyone realizing what is going on. I tackled him and tromped him in the ground. Yeah! I won.

We were just getting into rock-n-roll. Jan took a real liking to the oldies but goodies. In the seventh grade, we started going to the Bonita Vista Junior High dances. Neither Jan nor I did a lot of dancing. I guess it was all about the music and strobe lights. Jan was beginning to like boys, but those weren't the sort of things she talked over with a brother. I danced with a few girls, and Jan danced with her friends. There was one dance that I asked one of the dudes to dance with Jan. There was about ten feet between them, but Jan looked happy and that was the important thing.

Jan was still active in church and the Pathfinders. Pathfinders are very much like scouts only it was both boys and girls. Mom was the Pathfinder leader. They did a lot of trips and won honors. Dad was a Scout Master. He started when I was in the sixth grade but was discharged because a lot of sissy mothers didn't want their babies to get hurt. They wanted merit badges. Dad was more into rough games and camping.

Dad became Scout Master of a new troop. I came home late one night when we were supposed to receive our merit badges. I tried to get home after he left, because I didn't want to play Boy Scout anymore. Our patio was enclosed with a garage wall, a side of the house, and two sliding doors. As I walked through the door into the patio, Dad grabbed me, and slung me against the garage wall then bounced me off the other patio wall. He gave up on me and told me I'd always be worthless and never amount to a hill of beans. He said I wasn't anything but a quitter. I wondered what *he* had been all these years. He never finished college. He knew he was an A student but could only make a B because of being unable to be in front of a group. Jan and I went through that kind of stuff for the next ten years. Eventually, he abandoned all of us and got a divorce.

Dad spent a lot of his life behind the bedroom door. He would come home from work and that is where he went. He read out loud. He read geology books, and on Sabbath, he read the Bible. He would have been a great geologist or theologian. He believed in "spare the rod and spoil the child." Believe me, we were not spoiled, at least not by Dad.

*   *   *

In 1969, five of Jan's front teeth broke off. Mom and Dad took her to a dentist and x-rays showed that five of her roots had died. The dentist removed her front teeth and made her a permanent partial. In 1980, her permanent partial came loose and the same dentist x-rayed her and found the roots of the two teeth holding her partial had died. He made her another permanent partial with seven teeth on it.

Mom was working at the University California San Diego Hospital in the operating room. One day, she received a call from Jan that she had stuck her eye with a pin. Jan had not had her glasses on, and she had tried to remove a safety pin that was caught on her blouse. When the pin finally came loose, it stabbed her in the left eye. Mom told her supervisor she had to leave and why. She went home and took Jan to see her ophthalmologist. He ordered an x-ray, but the only x-ray department that could do the type of x-rays he wanted was at UCSD hospital. An ophthalmologist at UCSD looked at the x-ray, gave her an antibiotic to prevent infection, and referred her to her ophthalmologist after talking with him. She wore a patch on that eye for sometime.

One time Jan told Mom that her "butt hole" would fall out. Mom did not know what she was talking about until one day Jan was vomiting in the bathroom, and Mom walked in to check on her. Sure enough her rectum was hanging out about four inches. Mom took her to UCSD emergency room. They admitted her and kept examining her rectum. The residents could not find anything wrong. They were doing their exams with her lying on her side. They called in the chief professor, Dr. Scoma, and he had her hang her bottom off the bed and bear down. Out came her rectum. He performed surgery on her and put a Teflon band around her colon and, then attached it to her spinal column to prevent her rectum from prolapsing again. At the time of surgery, neurological tests showed some nerves in the pelvic area interchanged (bladder to rectum) with some being absent or not developed.

* * *

A lot of the kids I'd made friends with had fathers and/or brothers in the military. Some had already lost a brother or father to the Vietnam War. The atmosphere of this era had a big effect on us kids, especially living in the middle of so many military families. The kids began rebelling against being prohibited from doing what they wanted to do.

We decided we wanted change at our junior high school. We wanted to be able to have long hair, wear Levis and T-shirts. Most of the school dress codes required slacks and dress pants. It was time for a change, so the seventh, eighth, and ninth graders started having sit-ins. These were groups of adverse students, usually a global panel of people. Some of these students had already started growing their hair out or coming to school in Levis, and they were suspended on the spot. This went on for a while, until the school eventually let us vote on a dress code, and we actually won.

The eighth grade was hard for me so I convinced Mom and Dad to send me back to the academy. This was a major mistake due to poor grades, wrong friends, being easily influenced, and being vulnerable. Uncle Gene found out about my poor grades and tried to help me. I was having a history test the next day, and he was trying to help me study. Dad put in his words of wisdom, and told Uncle Gene he was wasting his time, that I could read, so just let me flunk out. Lucky for me everyone passed the test. Back in those years, the government's approach to drop-outs and those with poor grades was to get them through school. It was in the eighth grade that I became a cigarette junky and even found my way to alcohol pollution. Mom and Dad never knew the things I did. It wasn't until Mom found a case of beer under my bed that she knew. Mom was a trusting person and never thought her children would ever do anything they knew was wrong. She did not realize that it was about friends not ethics.

I was in trouble at the academy on a daily basis. The principle whom had been my third grade teacher was ashamed of me and couldn't understand how I went from a nice, sweet Sammy to this out-of-control young lad. In my mind, while in her office, I really didn't know either, but there was no turning back the clock. I was trapped. Jan, on the other hand stayed at Bonita Junior High, and her grades were good in spite of the way the other kids treated her. Maybe she had gotten used to all the nastiness and just ignored them.

When I was in the eighth grade my life took a total about face. Even I wasn't sure who I was. One time, I put a gun in my mouth, which was going to fix it all. I never had the nerve to pull the trigger. Thank God for that little bit of sanity.

At that time, my uncle Gene was living with us. He was still trying to finish college. He had changed. He was now a Buddha, a fanatical and had gotten caught up in a generation of druggies, peace, love, dope, long hair, a bandana, beads, sleeveless shirt, and Volkswagens, the whole hippie scene. I thought the beatnik generation was strange, but nothing like Uncle Gene. Little did I know I would be following in his tracks.

You may wonder why my parents let us get away with all of this. As I have said, Mom grew up being a trusting person and believed in everyone, so she was never suspicious until Gene called her one day and asked her if she had any diet pills that were not prescription. She did not, but he told her if she did to get rid of them just in case the cops came. Mom then became more aware of what was going on with him and his friends, but after all he was an adult. Even then she did not think I was a part of this.

Mom always cut my hair.

Dad would say "Sam, it's time for a haircut," and Mom would get out the clippers and go to work.

I decided I wanted to let my hair grow out like a lot of the other boys. My friend Charlie had run away from home because his military Dad forced him to have his hair cut.

One day, my Dad again said, "Sam it's time for a hair cut."

Mom knew I wanted to let my hair grow out, so she refused to cut it. Dad insisted she cut it or he would. Mom informed him she was not having her son run away from home over some dumb reason like not being able to have long hair. I let my hair grow out until I joined the Army, although I now have long hair again.

At home, I had acquired a lot of friends; swimming pools have a tendency to make that happen when it's hot. And money always helps. In the eighth grade, my friend Charlie went to Oregon, and when he returned he showed me all about drinking beer. That summer, Charlie and I learned about the weed, marijuana. The music we were all listening to was considered hard rock. Now, everyone uses it in the advertising or movies. Led Zeppelin or Black Sabbath, Rolling Stones, and Joe Walsh were just some of my favorites. Uncle Gene entertained my friends and me for awhile and then returned to Iowa.

One day, my friends and I were enjoying the pool. We had Steffen Wolf turned up as loud as it would go. Jan decided she wanted to watch TV, and she turned the stereo off. I came unglued and went in the house. I picked up a blown glass vase, about half-inch thick, and hit Jan as hard as I could on her arm. I thought I broke her arm.

She just shook her arm up and down saying "What did you do that for?"

I truly had no words. I knew I had blown it. What could I do? I knew Mom or Dad or both would most likely beat me to death. Some how, I managed to talk my way out of the situation or lied my way out. Anyway, I was getting worse in the way I was treating Jan. Linda was beginning to treat her badly too. There just didn't seem to be any space for being cool and being compassionate.

I wasn't at home much. Partying was the most important part of my life and would be for another seven years. I know Jan was doing better than I. She was still in church, something I had left back in the eighth grade. Then there was the swimming pool. If the weather would allow it, I don't believe she would ever have gotten out of the pool except to make dinner, eat, and go to the bathroom. I am ever so thankful that God remained with me. To this day, I have never understood why God never left me in spite of myself. Maybe Jan was praying for Linda and me.

One night I came home drunk and I sat down beside Mom on the sofa.

She said to me, "You stink, have you been drinking?"

I had to think of something, so I came up with the quickest answer I could, "No, but I smoke." Then the tears came. I don't know why or how, but Mom and I went outside and prayed in the yard. I felt God that night in my heart, but I just couldn't turn back.

The neighbor dudes and I used to play basket ball, racket ball, or volley ball at the Bonita High gym, which always gave us a good chance to drink without suspicions. Baseball and football also gave us opportunity to have a little alcohol. My life just kept reaching limits that would take me lower and lower. In ninth grade, parties were a way of life. I had no driver's license but could walk miles or hitchhike. My grades are no better, so I suggested that Mom and Dad let me go to Minnesota to work on Uncle Morris's farm.

*   *   *

Mom had then become Jan's guide, unlike the days gone by when Jan, Linda, and I used to play together and Linda or I would lead. Maybe Jan always needed a director, I don't know. At this stage, I had pretty much shunned and pushed her out of my life. I could not have her come between me and being cool, bad to the bone. Even so, I was still always looking over my shoulder ready to jump in and help her if someone treated her badly. They mostly were calling her names, but it was just as bad as getting beat on.

I wasn't at ninth grade graduation, so I don't know much about Jan or any events of the ninth graders or of Jan's summer. I had already gone to Minnesota to work on my Uncle Morris and Aunt Ruth's farm. I worked hard that summer baling hay and milking cattle. I never got to town and therefore, I couldn't get my hands on any alcohol or cigarettes. So I improvised, since in Minnesota there is a lot of road weed, hemp. I dried it and smoked it. It didn't taste real bad. I made $250 for the three months of work, and it didn't last long. Uncle Gene agreed to drive me back to San Diego, and that took care of fifty bucks.

Summer was over and it was time to start high school. Thank God, because junior high sucked. Jan and I started tenth grade, and without a doubt it was the best year of my life, but for Jan it was the beginning of a living hell. She started to want just a part of what Linda and I had. She wanted friends, the parties, and boyfriends. She wanted people to accept her.

As I entered my sophomore year, I started experimenting with acid, cocaine and heroin, you name it. My mind told me that I needed to stay away from these drugs, but they were totally likeable. I tried to stay with the drinking and weed. I began to entertain free love, sex, as a part of my development. I had become so delicate that I don't even know how I survived. I began going to concerts, a little smoke, a little acid, a little J.B., that's enough to kill anyone. I had left Jan so far behind on the side lines that I didn't even know she existed.

Linda and I were beginning to hang out together. Linda and I were both partying and leaving Jan out. Linda and her friends dated my friends, and I dated her friends. We all went to keggers together, on day trips to the beach, and we even covered for each other when we ditched school. We would answer the phone when the school called, and we forged Dad or Mom's name on our written excuses. We had filled out the school cards at the beginning of the year so our own hand-writing was on the cards and not Mom or Dad's. Linda began working in the school office so that made ditching school easier. A friend named Angie worked in the office my sophomore year, and she was good about covering for me.

When I would trip around Bonita High School, there would be Jan, sitting on a square planter box by herself or sometimes with a friend who was what we called "Smacko" (later on such kids were called Nerds).

One time, she yelled at me, "How come you never talk to me or say Hi? Can't you see me?"

It hurt. I wanted to hug her, but I strutted off, headed for a hot-boxed cigarette before class. I never forgot that day; Jan wanting to know why I didn't speak to her or acknowledge her. It was hard for me and I couldn't explain why, but I felt ashamed. I wanted to ask her how she was, but I just couldn't. I was hurting and saw her cry.

One of the girls she sat with that day was Gail, a girl I used to like at the academy. I didn't acknowledge her either, even though I had known her about eight years. I use to do things in the tenth grade that would most likely get me a jail sentence in this twenty-first century. The only reason I was in the tenth grade was because no one ever failed. Now, they try to say no child is left behind. I believe it is the same, just sounds better.

For me the '70s was another time of change. The 1970's music was changing from the protest music to hard rock to the disco-duck movement with Rod Stewart, Barry White, Barry Manilow, Captain & Tennille, and Paul Anka. Unlike the '60s it was a time when people didn't really have a cause. There were still the bands and artists that continued to speak of the dilemma of society, and were typically characterized by punk music.

The tenth grade ended, and summer was here. I spent my whole sophomore and junior years at the beach, surfing, body surfing, knee boarding. I lived for the waves, the drugs, alcohol, and sex. My friends and I went to the beach rain or shine, summer or winter. If we didn't have a ride we hitch-hiked. I started working my junior year loading shingles on roofs. It was hard work, but it was gas and alcohol money.

CHAPTER 8

Time of Change and Tribulation

Thinking about Jan and her eye sight, and how it must have been for her, I came up with an idea. Turn off all the lights in the house after dark and try to find your way to the bathroom with only the light of a full moon. Or, to simulate her depth perception, take a paper bag and put two little slits in the bag where your eyes are. Then try to reach for a glass of milk or try to place a glass of water on a small end table. It doesn't work well for me, so I know how hard it must have been for her. Jan was always quiet and distant from the rest of us. She had learned to utilize her vision so well that two psychologist who examined her could not believe her vision was 20/200.

I think Jan talked to our sister Linda and sometimes to Linda's friends or maybe other relatives. I don't know for sure, but Jan and I didn't talk.

I got my driver's license in the tenth grade, and I was never home. Jan always wished she could drive, and maybe it would have given her more freedom, more of an equal edge that we all had. I'm quite sure it would have, basically because it would have meant that she wasn't blind. That would have changed all kinds of things, but it just wasn't the case. It seemed like Jan began to fight with herself over the hand that God dealt her.

*   *   *

In the eleventh grade, things began to change for Jan. In her mind she wanted to have a life like Linda and I. She started ditching school, as Linda and I did. Finally, she quit school just after her eighteenth birthday. Her friends kept asking me why she wasn't in school. They thought she was sick. I didn't want to say she quit because that wasn't a good thing, but what could I say?

Jan became angry at Mom because she did not want Jan to drop out of school. Jan walked to the supermarket, which was a mile away and bought some cigarettes. When she came home she sat down beside Mom on the sofa so Mom would smell it. Mom was very hurt and told her she could not smoke in the house. It was a bad habit for Jan, and she started smoking one right after another.

Shortly after Jan quit school, she ran away from home, and this was the start of a whole new Jan. Unfortunately, it was not a good Jan. I do understand what it is like to want to be accepted and equal, to be part of society. Jan would go to down town San Diego to a park where drunks and homeless hung out, and she would get drunk. One time, she went to the Oceanside Marine base with a black dude she had met in downtown San Diego. She was gone a couple of days. Mom and Dad were worried about her, but had no idea where to look for her. Then late one evening, she called home for Mom to come get her. She needed help and someone to talk to. Mom worked from 11:00 p.m. to 7:00 a.m. at the hospital and could not go, so she told Dad to go get Jan.

Dad made me go after her, so my friend Charlie went with me to get her. I was seventeen years old, and I was afraid for Jan. I was afraid for us. I was trying to deal with the unknown factors, black men, Marines, druggies, rapists, women beaters and who knew what else. Charlie and I drove two hours to a place that we knew nothing about and had no idea what to expect. We were pretty sure we might have to fight these guys. The ride was a quiet one. Charlie was as unsure about this event as I was.

We finally arrived at the Oceanside bus stop. My heart was beating a thousand times a minute. I was scared to death, but there was Jan standing outside waiting. She was so stoned she could hardly talk or stand up. She looked horrible, I mean real horrendous. She was crying, not like you or I, but more of a scream or yelling, but crying. I tried to get her to come home but she refused. She just wanted someone to talk to. She really wanted Mom and didn't understand why Dad sent me. I tried to talk to her. I tried to understand. The whole situation had tears coming from my eyes. I didn't understand all of this. I began to understand as she told me what she was all about. For the first time, I was listening, and it hurt.

In my life I'm not sure I ever experienced a sadder life-awakening moment. In spite of how I was feeling, I listened to her unload and determined she was going to go home with Charlie and me. All at once, she began to tell me how much these guys loved her and understood her. They treated her like she was someone, not just a blind, disabled, ugly person. It really set me off to think these devious, brutal, vial Marines had used and raped my sister who was a poor defenseless, blind girl and easy prey. These Marines had taken total advantage of my sister. I was ready to kill. I became angry, but she wouldn't get in the car. She ran back into the bus stop, where these dudes were. I was scared for her. Anyway, Jan wouldn't leave so Charlie and I started home.

On the way home, I was angry and didn't know what Dad would say because Jan wasn't with us. Charlie didn't know what to say.

When I walked in the door without Jan, Dad said, "Just let her go. If she calls again I will go with you."

He said he should have gone to get her. I was crying for Jan as I talked to Mom about all this. Neither one of us understood. I was really afraid for her. In my mind I could only imagine finding her dead or getting a call from the police that they found her dead body. Mom and I prayed as we usually did when we got caught up in situations that were out of our control.

Jan called again; my heart raced. Maybe this time those Marines would be waiting for us. I even thought about taking a weapon.

Then Dad said, "Let's go. I'm going with you this time. I'll show you how it's done."

All the way to Oceanside, all kinds of thoughts were in my head, thank God none of which came true. When we arrived at the bus station we had to go inside this time and get Jan to come out to the car. Dad told her we just wanted to talk to her by the car.

Then all at once Dad opened the door and threw Jan in the car and said "Now take off. Drive."

Jan was kicking, screaming, and saying things that were totally untrue. Things like "you don't love me," "you treat me like a retard", "you never make me feel wanted", "you never treat me like you do Linda and Sam" and "you can take me home, but I'll just run away again."

A lot of what Jan was saying maybe was true, but it hurt even though it was the drugs and alcohol talking. Sometimes, drugs and alcohol become the truth. When we got home Jan slept it off and Mom booked her an appointment with a psychiatrist. Life went back the way it was for a while. Everyone just sort of let it go. Linda and I went back to partying with our peers and school buds.

*   *   *

While all this was going on, Jan had become pregnant. Mom did not believe in abortions, but she did not feel with all Jan's drinking that Jan was capable of raising a child. Mom felt she couldn't cope with the issue and did not want to take on the responsibility of raising another child who might be handicapped, so she encouraged Jan to have an abortion. Mom has since wondered if it would have changed Jan by having someone to love and care for.

Jan started working on becoming a certified nurse assistant. She rode back and forth from Chula Vista to National City with Dad. One day, the instructor of the CNA class called Mom to tell her the class was too big and she needed to screen a few of the students out. She had decided Jan would be one of them. Jan's grades were excellent, and Mom begged the instructor not to eliminate Jan, but the teacher did not think Jan could handle feeding and helping disadvantaged children where the students would be getting their clinical experience. Mom told her this would emotionally ruin Jan as she wanted to be a CNA so bad. Never-the-less, the teacher discharged her. Needless to say Mom was right, it made Jan feel like she could not do anything. That night, riding home with Dad, Jan told him what happened.

He said, "Your mother should never have made you take the CNA course anyway."

He never recognized it was Jan's desire to become a CNA and that Mom gave her encouragement.

*   *   *

I was beginning to use any drug I could get a hold of. I took "window paine" (a form of LSD) once and watched an Alice Cooper concert for three hours that was really an hour show. Luckily, I didn't die on that one. I had just gone through the worst of my life, so why was I doing what I really hated? It was the same thing I had just seen Jan go through. Maybe it was guilt or a death wish, I really don't know.

The next year, my senior year, I quit school, which was a major mistake. I loaded roofs with shingles full time and hated it. Charlie wanted to join the army. It sounded good to me and would be better than loading roofs. Every day, all the guys were checking their draft numbers. Dad had no problem with me going in the Army, but Mom said absolutely not. Since I was not eighteen, Dad signed for me to go in the army with my buddy Charlie. I spent two years in the army. When I came home things had changed.

Those so-called friends were not friends anymore, and the people I partied with had changed too. I tried to fit in, but it just wasn't the same. The public wasn't respectful to the military; they called us "Baby Killers" or just spit on us.

Shortly after I joined the army Dad decided to divorce the family. He just wanted his freedom. Relatives had never thought Mom and Dad's marriage would last. They thought he married her so she would give him sons since Mom came from a family of seven brothers. Too bad, all he got was me. He didn't realize it is the male who determines the sex of the fetus.

This divorce set Jan back. She thought it was because of her, especially since Dad thought she was not normal and not capable to do anything worthwhile or able to live by herself. If only Dad could have encouraged us, instead of blaming everything on his upbringing. He had great parents, but because they had rules, he never could see how caring they were.

Dad had given Mom an African violet, and it sat in the kitchen window. Mom had a way with violets. After Dad moved out, the violet began to die. Jan told Mom that even the violet was sad and dying because Dad left. Mom found out that Jan was over-watering the violet, and that was why it died.

Jan contacted the California Department of State employment for the disabled. Jan wanted to be seen for what she knew and could do, not as a weird-looking girl who knew nothing, but the government stereotyped everyone, which may be why equal opportunity just isn't in America. They thought since she wanted a job that she could make potholders. Come on, she was legally blind not an invalid or stupid. She would catch the bus on our street, change buses in downtown Chula Vista and ride it to downtown San Diego. Jan was smart and was soon fed up with making potholders. She wanted to do something that interested her and that she would enjoy doing, so she quit her job. She was able to get on disability after that. The government needs to wake up and assure "no child is left behind." The government needs to see people for who they are and not just their color, sex, or physically handicapped.

Jan got her own apartment so she could be independent. It was a good idea, but it made it easier for her to get drunk. Her drinking would last for days and weeks on end. She would drink wine by the gallon, never eating or sleeping. She would usually hurt herself by falling down, tripping over something in her apartment, or burn her face while lighting a cigarette from the stove. She was attracting all kinds of bums who were using her for a free drink and borrowing her disability money which they never paid back.

She began seeing a psychiatrist and was in and out of the Twinkie farm, like the psych unit had a revolving door. Then she would go through periods of peace and tranquility. But something would set her off, and it would start all over. The drinking got so bad that even I couldn't stand it. I was beginning to slow down drinking myself, because I would see her drunker than a skunk or I would have to take her to the emergency room. It totally made me sick. I became even more embarrassed to have her around or to be seen with her.

Her looks were becoming disgusting. She weighed about eighty-five or ninety pounds and was five foot six. Her face was all scarred, and her clothes never looked like they fit.

After the divorce, Mom worked two jobs and was working on her bachelor's degree in order to keep her sanity, so she didn't have a lot of time to be with Jan. Our sister Linda got an apartment in Coronado and cut Jan out of her life.

Three years after the divorce Mom decided she wanted to live at the beach and rented her house to my friend Charlie and his wife Debbie. Mom wanted time with her friends, time to herself, without having Jan depend on her. It was a good deal for a while, but we all knew it wouldn't last. Jan couldn't let go, She was determined Mom wasn't going to get rid of her. This wasn't Mom's intention at all. She knew Jan needed the security and support she got from Mom, but Mom had just wanted Jan to learn to be as independent as possible and for both of them to have their own lives.

Jan was living with Charlie and Debbie in Mom's house. It seemed like a good idea. That way Jan would remain in a familiar environment she grew up in, with friends, someone she had known like a brother since sixth grade. For a while it was okay, and then her drinking caught up with her. Charlie had children, and he was afraid she might hurt one of them. I tried to get Jan to control herself, but it didn't happen. Jan then got an apartment, close to the hospital.

*   *   *

Nineteen seventy nine was a busy year. I had bought a townhouse and was living in it, but I had to sell it because I had too much debt, so I rented my first apartment. Linda and I met on a blind date arranged by a good friend. Linda went to Bonita High after I did and she lived in Bonita, California. The ironic part of our meeting is we were at the beach and Linda and her friend thought it would be funny if I went into the women's bathroom instead of the men's. Unknown to me there was a young girl in the bathroom. She did not think it was funny at all. She had me arrested and I was charged with public drunkenness and went to jail. Thank God because this girl wanted to file a rape charge.

This started Linda and I on a meaningful relationship and we had so much in common. It must have been in the cards, because we were married two years later on Valentine's Day. One might think I married my sister, since Linda Davis and my sister Linda have the same name and birthday, but Linda, my wife is three years younger than my sister. At first they didn't even like each other. Jealousy I believe. After my sister Linda and Robert Duncan were married the two Linda's became good friends.

After I married Linda, my beautiful wife, I realized my past had to change and with a son on the way I needed to make changes in my life. I wanted my own business and needed to stop taking drugs and alcohol. I took the test for roofing and got my license then started my own roofing company. Later on I taught roofing at City College in San Diego, California. I taught the students about the different types of shingles, how to measure, and how to do estimates. I kept busy and loved my work.

I have to wonder why Linda married into such a mixed up family. I thank God that Linda is as loving, kind, understanding, and most of all forgiving as any one person can be. Linda never treated Jan as if she were different or disabled, only as a person, a sister-in-law.

It was that year that Grandpa Jones discovered he had intestinal cancer, which metastasized to his liver. Mom and Sister Linda drove to Iowa to be with him and Grandma when he came home from the hospital after his surgery.

When they returned home Mom learned from the emergency room nurses that Jan had gone to the ER everyday complaining about the catheter she had in her bladder.

She had problems urinating and the urologist had looked in her bladder and determined she never completely emptied her bladder and therefore her bladder muscles were weak, causing her to have problems urinating. He had put the catheter in hoping that by keeping her bladder empty, her muscles would become elastic again. She had an appointment with the urologist after Mom got home from Iowa. He scoped her bladder and told Mom if he had not looked in her bladder previous to the catheter, he would have thought she had cancer, but since he had scoped her bladder earlier he determined she was allergic to the latex in the catheter. Everyone had thought her ER trips were due to loneliness and needing Mom's reassurance and support, but she really did have a problem.

Another great event was the birth of my son, Dustin. Mom took a trip to Hawaii with her friend Mary Ann, and since Dustin was her first grandchild, she brought him several things from Hawaii. She loved shopping for him. Jan was okay while Mom was gone to Hawaii. Maybe having a new nephew gave her some consolation.

Jan was having problems with her sinuses. The doctor told Mom that Jan had a deviated septum and needed surgery. The surgery was apparently successful, except the stitches under her nose came out before the skin was healed. Medicaid said it was cosmetic and would not pay to have it repaired, and Mom could not afford to pay for the surgery. Now this poor girl, who already had facial problems, had another defect added to her looks. She had a gap where the stitches had been, causing her nose to flatten.

Jan took a cooking class for restaurant work. She worked at the Community Center helping to cook and serve a hundred seniors each day. She eventually quit as she had to walk to work in the dark, and this frightened her. She liked helping people, so Mom suggested she volunteer at Paradise Valley Hospital. This helped prevent some of her drinking. She worked as a volunteer sometimes forty hours a week. She did volunteer work for several years and really enjoyed it. She especially enjoyed helping the elderly. In May 1983 she was awarded a "Carnation Community Service Silver Awards" bowl in cooperation with the Volunteer Action Center of San Diego, a division of United Way,

When Charlie and Debbie moved out of Mom's house, Mom moved back into her own house. This would make it less stressful for Mom to be available for Jan since the house was closer to where Jan lived than Mom's beach apartment.

CHAPTER 9

Change Is Not Always Good

M om liked school and was always working to better her education. She went to college and got a masters in business administration. Grandpa Jones died March 1983. In August of that year Mom was hired as the director of nurses in a small hospital in Calhoun, Georgia. She wanted to see if Jan could be independent and care for herself. They agreed that Jan would live in her apartment in National City for a year, and then, if she wanted she could move to Georgia.

Jan tried to depend on Dad to help her, but he just wasn't there like Mom, so her drinking resumed. Things had gotten bad, and at the beginning of 1984, Mom sent Jan a ticket to come to Georgia. Dad shipped some of her records, clothes, and what-ever he thought she might need or want. Everyone realized that Mom and Jan would be together for the rest of their lives and that Jan would always need Mom's love, friendship, reassurance, encouragement, and support.

Mom's house was three mile from town and on two acres. There were no houses close by and so no neighbors with whom Jan could become acquainted. Jan was good for a while, but boredom caught up with her and she started drinking. Mom came home from work one evening to find out Jan had gotten drunk and fallen off the back step of the carport injuring her ribs and right elbow. Several days later, her elbow was swollen, and she complained of pain when she breathed. Mom took her to the doctor and found out she had cellulitis in her elbow from the injury. Her ribs were broken and had punctured her lung. She had to have a tube put in her chest. She was in the hospital until the fluid on her lungs was gone. Jan never made any friends in Georgia. Probably what Jan enjoyed most in Georgia was going to Atlanta to eat at their favorite Mexican restaurant.

Grandma Jones loved to visit them in Georgia. Jan enjoyed going sightseeing with Mom and Grandma, even though Jan could not see very much out the car window and what she did see was a blur. They loved going to Amicalola Falls, the Bavarian Alpine Village, and Stone Mountain Georgia with the carvings of veterans of the Confederacy from the Civil War. When they walked around these areas, Jan could get closer and see a bit more.

Mom and Jan decided take Grandma to visit Uncle Cliff and Jolene who lived in Panama City, Florida. They thought they would surprise them, so they did not let them know they were coming. When they got there, they discovered Uncle Cliff and Jolene had recently moved back to Missouri. Jan, Mom, and Grandma enjoyed the weekend on the beach, even though Cliff no longer lived there.

* * *

After she had been in Georgia for three years, the Adventist Health System tried to recruit Mom to move to Manchester, Kentucky, as director of nursing at Manchester Memorial Hospital. Mom was not sure she wanted to move to the hills of Kentucky. One night, Mom had a dream she had gone to Manchester for an interview.

The next morning, Jan told Mom, "I think you should call Tom and go to Kentucky for an interview."

This happened again the next night, and Mom decided maybe God was directing this, so she called Tom Amos the CEO and set up an interview.

Mom and Jan moved to Kentucky in November just before Thanksgiving. Everyone who worked in the hospital (who was not a native of Manchester) lived on Hospital grounds. Mom and Jan lived in a six-apartment complex. Others lived in mobile homes or condos. What a difference it was for them living in the hills of Kentucky. The mountain out their living-room window was black with coal. But when spring came, that same mountain was beautiful with dogwood trees in bloom. The people who lived in Manchester knew Mom and Jan cared about people or they wouldn't be there.

Jan has always loved to cook and bake. She would start baking cookies and making candy before Thanksgiving and continue until after the New Year. She would always give my family and my sister Linda's family a big can of her baked goods for the holidays. Since we now lived across the United States from her, she gave them to the people in the apartment building and to others who lived in hospital housing.

One summer Dick, the personnel manager, asked Jan if she would like some cucumbers from his garden. She said she would, so she could make some pickles. Dick said his wife, Shirley, didn't like pickles so she never made any. Jan made up pints of pickles and gave some to Dick. Shortly after that, the dietary department needed a part-time employee. Dick told Larry, the director of the dietary department to hire Jan. This was the first time in her life that anyone except Mom recognized her abilities and talents. Mom was surprised when Jan stopped by her office after completing the paperwork to tell Mom she had the job. Mom asked her what job and she said "in the kitchen." Mom knew nothing about this but was so happy for Jan.

There were times Jan would work fourteen days straight as a part-time worker. She loved her job and would kid around with the other employees. One day, she was cleaning the counter, and another lady told her she had already cleaned it. Jan asked her if she ever felt where she cleaned as it still had dirty stuff on it. The only way Jan could tell if it was clean was by the feel. Another time, one of the dietary staff asked her why she worked so much. Jan's response was "money, money, money." Everyone laughed, as they knew Jan could care less how much money she had as long as she had enough to meet her needs.

Kentucky was a lovely place to live and a place our family loved to visit. Mom and Jan loved company and loved showing them the area. You could visit several states in one day because the states are close together in that area. You could stand astride two state lines and climb mountains, crawl into caves, and walk across gorges. Grandma Jones at age eighty crawled into a cave in Clay County, Kentucky with Mom and Jan to see some Indian writings. They enjoyed going to Levi Jackson State Park in London and Cumberland Falls with the famous nighttime moon bow near Corbin. One time, Aunt Dorothy and her children, Richard, Melinda, and Wesley went to visit. They went to Cumberland Gap and climbed the mountain. Wes and Melinda were so excited because they stood on the states of Kentucky and Virginia with Jan. Mom has always been sorry that my family could never visit.

Mom and Jan liked going to Lexington to the Horse Park. Mom's assistant director of nursing, Shirley, was a New Yorker. One time, Mom and Jan went to a restaurant with Dick and Shirley and were telling them about their day at the Horse Park.

Shirley said to her husband Dick, in her heavy New York accent, "Why don't we go to the Hoss Pauk?"

Dick told Shirley, "When you learn to say 'Horse Park' we will go."

Jan cracked up. I'm not sure they ever went.

Mom and Jan would go to Iowa to visit Grandma Jones and family. One time when they were going, they took the dietitian's son, Mark, with them since his grandparents lived in Iowa. Mom was stopped by a cop for speeding. Mom told the cop she had her cruise control set on sixty-eight.

He told her "In this state, the speed limit is sixty-five so slow down."

He didn't give her a ticket, but everyone at the hospital heard about it, thanks to Mark and Jan.

*   *   *

Three years after moving to Kentucky, the District CEO decided to let Mom go. To this day she does not know why. Jan continued to work and paid the rent until Mom found another job. They moved from Kentucky to Orlando, Florida.

Jan had to give up her job in Kentucky when they moved. Mom wanted Jan to be able to work, but the Florida hospital only wanted her to volunteer. It seemed like they were profiling her and only saw what she looked like, not what she had done in Kentucky. Our society has become good at profiling not just the disadvantaged but also the aged and certain ethnic groups.

Jan was not happy since she no longer had a job. Mom worked in the emergency room at Apopka, Florida. Her long time friend Eva lived nearby in Florida, and Mom bought a house in the same housing area.

Don, who had been friends with Jan growing up in California, also lived in the area. Needless to say, the drinking started again. Jan and Don would go to the park and drink, or go to one of their homes since both moms worked. They would sit out in the yard and imbibe their alcohol.

Jan and Mom got involved in ceramics and Mom bought a kiln and some molds from a warehouse that was going out of business. This helped Jan occupy some of her time, but it did not stop her drinking. Mom had been doing ceramics off and on since 1960, and she and Jan took some classes to learn new ways to paint and decorate ceramics.

Then one day, Mom fell off a ladder in the garage and crushed her knee. Mom was happy Jan was living with her as the doctor told Mom she was to stay in bed for two weeks, until she had surgery and then would not be able to take care of herself. Mom was off work for six months. They were grateful for their ceramics. When Mom went back to work she was transferred to the preoperative room in Florida Hospital in Orlando, Florida which was 1,200-bed hospital. She did not enjoy her job there.

Mom and Jan thought Florida was beautiful with all the lakes and the fun things to do. They enjoyed the beach, Disney World, riding the airboats, eating out at the Olive Garden, and going to the Botanical Gardens. The beach was so much warmer than the Pacific Ocean, but they lived farther away from the beach than they had in California, so they did not go there as much as they would have liked.

I'm not sure if Jan's drinking was the result of jealousy, being uprooted again and again, or because she found it easy to do what she felt was essential when Mom wasn't around. Mom would go on singles retreats to help those who might need counseling and women's retreats to make friends. Jan would never go with her, but in Jan's eyes Mom wasn't about to do anything without Jan. Jan always seemed to find a way to get control of Mom. It was usually getting drunk and then hurting herself, which resulted in Mom having to come to her aid.

CHAPTER 10

Home at Last

In March 1991 Mom went to California to her nursing Alumni Reunion. Her previous Director of Nurses was doing home health and suggested mom interview for a job since West Health Care, a branch of Paradise Valley Hospital, was opening an office in North San Diego County. Lil thought that since Linda and Bob lived in Temecula, California and my family lived in Ramona she would be close to her family. West HealthCare called her a couple of weeks later regarding the job. The new office would open in one month. She gave a three week notice even though she had not really been hired. Mom was ready to go. Mom and Jan lived in Florida two years before moving back to California where they lived in our fifth wheel in Ramona, California until Mom decided where she wanted to live.

Mom rented an old house in Escondido and they moved into it. One night after they moved into the house Jan got up and went outside for a cigarette. There was an earthquake. She woke mom and ask her if she was going to get up. Mom told her there was nothing she could do about it so no she was going to stay in bed. Jan decided mom was right so she went back to bed. The next morning we learned the quake was a 6.7 in the Los Angeles area.

One time after mom moved to Escondido, she was attending a nursing convention and had to leave town for a few days. I stopped by one day to see how Jan was doing. She had burned her face on the stove lighting a cigarette. She was crawling around on the floor.

I asked why, and she said, "I think I broke my leg."

I said, "Why didn't you call someone for help?"

She told me she did, but they wanted her to go to detox and she didn't want to go. She had been out watering the lawn and in her drunken clumsiness she got the garden hose wrapped around her leg. It some-how yanked her off her feet. She was so drunk she didn't know how badly she was injured and that her leg was broken. She had broken both bones in her left leg. She had to have major surgery and a rod put in her leg. She was laid up for several months. She could not get out to buy her liquor and seemed okay for awhile. There was a small store next to where they lived, and as soon as Jan was able, she would hobble over to the store and buy what she wanted.

Mom bought a condo in Escondido, and Jan decided she wanted to live alone. Jan found a mobile home near a supermarket and moved in. She met a guy living next door. Her TV started giving her problems. She called the cable company, but the so-called friend illegally hooked up to her cable. He was a moocher and would con her out of money, cigarettes, food, alcohol, and anything he wanted. Sometime later he hooked up to her cable again.

By this time she had gotten wise to his con artistry and told him, "You're nothing but a gigolo so get out of here and go back east where you belong."

He knew he was done and moved.

She had begun drinking again. The liquor store was just a block down the street. She bought more alcohol than I could have drunk in a year. She drank a case of Jack Daniels and a gallon of wine all in a week or less. Every time Mom was gone, I would get a call, which I always resented. One time the call came from the sheriff's department. Jan was extremely drunk and had hurt herself and was bothering the people who lived in the mobile park. I had had enough. First I chewed Jan out. Then I took her to the liquor store and showed them my sister. I told them at the store that if they ever sold her another bottle of alcohol I would be suing them for aiding Jan in her self-destruction or suicide. They said she was over twenty-one and they could sell to whomever they wished. I should have told them she was not a responsible person. Now days in some states you cannot sell alcohol to someone so drunk that they might hurt themselves.

Having had enough of Jan's self-inflicted, suicidal craziness, Linda and I drove her to Paradise Valley Hospital. We thought that if we took her there where she knew most of the people, they could help. We had grown up with these people and gone to church with them. We went to the emergency room. I wanted her admitted to the psychiatric unit to protect her from herself. They refused to admit her because she wouldn't sign in. This really angered me. I told them to look at her. If they could not see she was suicidal, then what was it? I told them that I was her brother, and she needed help, we all need help, but to no good. She had to admit to them that she wanted to harm herself, and she won't say a word. Mom and I have never understood why they didn't admit her under Section 5150 of the California Code, which allows for involuntary admission, and they could have held her for seventy-two hours.

Now I know why there are so many junkies on the street WAKE UP AMERICA.

Again, Linda and I had gotten through another episode of "Jan's Guiding Light," a routine soap opera that happened when ever Mom needed to leave town and couldn't take Jan with her.

Aunt Sharon came to visit Mom from Iowa, and she wanted to visit Jan. They arrived at Jan's mobile home to find her with her hair burned and her face with second-degree burns from lighting a cigarette on the stove. Mom took her to the University of California at San Diego hospital emergency room, and they admitted her to the hospital. She was very lucky as she had very little scarring this time due to the medication and the type of dressings used, or maybe because of all the other scarring it didn't look as bad.

In 1994, Jan's permanent dental partial was giving her trouble. They lived in Escondido so she went to a new dentist. When he saw her partial was loose he decided to pull all her teeth and make her full dentures. He never discussed this with Jan or Mom and no one knows if he even did x-rays. Mom was never happy with him, as she did not know if all of Jan's roots had died or he just wanted more money. Later on, Jan had more trouble and could not keep her dentures in, even with denture glue. She saw an oral surgeon in Escondido. He did x-rays and learned that her maxillary sinuses, which should be pin-point size, were enlarged to the size of a dime and her bones were deteriorating. He referred her to UCLA to the dental clinic. They did all kinds of tests and determined that there was not much they could do. They discussed surgery, but because the bone in her jaw was deteriorating they did not think it would help. They discussed taking a bone from another location and transplanting it into her jaw, but they were not sure the blood supply was sufficient to let it grow and heal.

*   *   *

Mom loved home-health nursing and would sometimes drive a hundred miles a day, just to see five patients. One thing that disturbed her was going to a small, residential-care home, then called a "board and care," to find all the clients asleep with the TV on and no caregiver around. She decided when she retired she would open a loving residential-care facility. One day, a real-estate company left a flyer on her door. She looked through it and in the middle was an estate home for sale at $205,000. The house had been vacant for a year. It was perfect for a residential-care facility. Mom made an offer of $165,000, and the seller came back with $165,500. Who was going to fight over $500?

When escrow closed, Mom went to San Diego Community Services to learn what the requirements were for opening and running a board and care facility for Seniors. Since I owned a construction company, I made the required changes to meet regulations. Windows in the three bedrooms were changed to doors, since the residents had to be able to get out of their rooms in case of fire. The fire department approved a deck to be built fifty feet from the house with a walkway from the bedrooms. I added ramps to the back and front doors for wheel chair accessibility. My brother-in-law Bob, checked out the electric.

Mom continued with her nursing. She planned for Jan to move in and help run the facility, since Jan loved elderly people and liked to cook. Jan understood she would not be able to drink and had stopped when Mom bought the house. She also understood she could not smoke in the house. By the time we had the house ready for inspection by the state; Mom had taken the forty-hour administrator course. She was licensed and opened the facility on January 5, 1995. They got their first client in mid-January 1995. Mom did not like calling the facility a board and care and licensed it as Rolling Knolls Residential Care for the Elderly. She wrote the State of California and told them "board and care" was for animals and she was caring for the elderly. The state changed all licenses from "Board and Care" to "Residential Care for the Elderly."

This was the best thing that ever happened to Jan. She had a home that was hers, and a job that she loved. All these elderly people were Jan's family that she never had and her friends that she had never made. This was the dawn of a new life that my sister Jan had always dreamed of; to be someone equal, to belong, and to be loved. Jan took care of these residents as if they were her children. When one of these people passed on it was hard on Jan. She lost a friend, a family member, and part of her new found life.

No one was allowed in her kitchen. Jan had things in a particular place where she knew where they were. I never understood why, until Uncle David told me a story about when Jan was visiting Grandma Jones.

Grandma said to Jan, "Look whose here."

Jan didn't respond. Then Dave said hello to Jan, and she responded to his voice. He was across the room from her, and she couldn't tell who he was until he spoke to her. That's when Dave knew that Jan's vision was next to zero. With Jan being legally blind, if anything in the kitchen was out of place, she would be lost and break things trying to find where it was. Whenever I visited, she always kept my coffee cup in a certain place. It never made sense to me, but I understand now.

Lots of people believed Mom pushed Jan into doing everything, whether she wanted to or not. I thank God Mom did encourage her, or Jan may never have had a chance. Jan truly would have been a dependent invalid, maybe even have killed herself. Finally, Jan was doing what she was born to do and loving it. She was the boss and caring for people who needed her and loved her.

Their first client, Ray, was in his eighties and had confined himself to a wheel-chair even though he could get around well with a walker. Jan thought he needed exercise, so she would sit in his wheel-chair and have him push her from the back patio to the deck and back. The kitchen had an open bar separating the dining room and TV area from the kitchen. The residents could always see Jan since she spent most of her time in the kitchen cooking and baking.

By September, they had six residents, two men and four ladies. They were licensed for six people, two people to a room. Mom had learned over the years of dealing with other RCFE's that if two compatible people were in one room they became friends and did not feel alone.

Their second client, Gladys had a stroke and was paralyzed on the left side. She was in a wheel chair. Gladys would watch Jan work and was never critical. But Jan thought Gladys was being like the kids she went to school with and was making fun of her. This really bothered Jan, even though Mom tried to help her understand that Gladys did like her and thought she was a hard worker and maybe was envious. Mom and Jan, being ceramists, taught Gladys how to paint ceramics. Gladys wanted to know the entire technique, how the ceramics were poured, cleaned, and fired. She was really amazed at all the work that went into doing ceramics. Gladys was on dialysis and Mom would take her to and from the dialysis clinic three times a week.

When Lester came to live with them he was in a wheel-chair. He could assist with helping himself in and out of the chair to the sofa, bed, or toilet, but could not walk. At age seventy-four Lester had been diagnosed with a disease that affected his walking, and the doctors at Mayo Clinic felt they could not do anything to help him due to his age. He was eighty-three years old when he came to live with Jan and Mom. On his ninety-second birthday, Jan baked him a cake and bought wax numbers to put on it. She turned the numbers around to read "29" to make him feel good.

Mom bought a twelve-passenger van and had the back-seat taken out and a lift put in so she could take the clients on weekly excursions around the county. Jan would prepare food, and they would go on picnics. They would drive to Imperial Beach, up the Silver Strand and then across the Coronado Bridge and home to Escondido, or they would go to Valley Center and watch the ducks on the lake. By the time they were done with their outing, everyone was ready for a nap.

Mom decided Jan should become the administrator so Mom could go back to nursing. Jan attended the forty-hour class but was afraid she would not pass the exam. Dad did not think she could pass it either. Mom reviewed things with Jan as she drove her to take her exam. Jan passed with a ninety-six percent on her test. She was so excited she called Dad to let him know she passed. She and Mom took classes on an annual basis because every two years they had to have forty continuing education credits to renew their administrative certificates.

Linda and I had moved our family to Colorado in 1995 due to a recession in California. Also California allowed a flood of illegal's in which caused a drop in wages and my earnings went down. As a business person you need a firm price for your product and I wasn't able to charge enough to make a profit. The only way I could compete was to follow the example of other contractors, which was hire illegal help at ten dollars an hour. I just could not bring myself to cheating my American friends by taking away their work and giving the job to someone from another country. So I closed my business for a job offer with a construction company in Colorado. December 1995, I went to Colorado to work for T.L. Roofing. It didn't work out. I didn't get the job position I was promised. I should have gone back to California, but I liked Colorado so I opened my own business and moved my family to Mancos, Colorado. Since I was working mostly in the Western Slope area, I moved my family to Grand Junction, Colorado.

Sometimes, when Mom was coming to visit us or to go to Iowa to a family reunion, she would bring Jan with her. Mom would hire a girl to stay twenty-four hours a day to care for the residents. She would have an administrator friend be on call while they were gone out of town.

Dad never gave Jan much credit for anything she did. One time when he was visiting, Mom called home to let Jan know she was on her way home from work. Dad answered the phone. He asked Mom if she knew how much work Jan did. Mom assured him she knew Jan knocked herself out cleaning, cooking, laundry, watering the yard, and the fruit trees on the hill. She told him if it wasn't for Jan she would have to quit work or close the facility. About the only thing Mom did at home was get the residents up in the morning for breakfast, and at bedtime she helped Jan put them to bed. Jan did not like showering other people so Mom hired girls to shower the clients. Mom and Jan would take the clients out for a drive on weekends.

Grandma Jones was eighty-six years old when she came to live with Jan and Mom. Grandma loved visiting with Gladys and Ray. They would sit out on the patio and visit. Ray had lived in Canada and so had Grandma, so they had things to talk about. Most of the other clients would sit inside and watch TV unless Jan brought them out on the patio. She had Mom record some old-time music and some popular music. She would exercise with the residents and would dance with them. There was a hill behind the house that had orange and plum trees on it. Jan would go up on the hill and water the trees. Everyone sat on the patio and watched her.

In 1997, my cousin, Becki, and her six-month-old daughter, Ivana, came from Iowa to live with Mom and Jan. Jan loved having Ivana to care for, which was something she had never experienced before. When Ivana was two years old, Becki met Tim Boock and one year later they were married and moved into their own apartment. Ivana never knew her biological Dad, and he never paid child support. Since Becki worked, Jan still baby-sat Ivana until Becki and Tim moved to Apple Valley, California.

Jan was a loving person, but she was not a hugger. One time, Grandma told Jan she want to give her a hug. She told Grandma she didn't need a hug. Grandma was good with using reverse psychology, so after that she would tell Jan "Grandma needs a hug" and Jan would hug her and Grandma could hug Jan. Mom also adapted this approach so she could hug Jan. Grandma died in January 1998 at age eighty-eight.

Winnie came to live with Mom and Jan in 1998. Winnie had no family of her own, and she became like family. She and Jan did a lot of things together. They loved going to the Palm Springs Follies, Encinitas Flower Gardens, Wild Animal Park, the zoo, and many other places. Winnie was two years older than Mom. She could not do much but helped Jan with what she could. One July, they came to visit us in Colorado. We rented cabins at Mesa Lake for the weekend. It was a great weekend. Everyone, except Winnie and Jan, went down to the lake. Jan enjoyed the chipmunks and whistle pigs as she could get close enough to see them.

My son, Dustin, wanted to graduate with his Ramona, California, friends, so he went to live with Mom and Jan too. This was another person in Jan's life who was irreplaceable for her and whom she loved. He delivered pizza after school. He would frequently bring home left-over pizzas. Jan loved having him bring home pizzas, because it meant she didn't have to worry about what was for lunch the next day.

CHAPTER 11

Hardship and Sorrow

Jan began having health problems. Some of her illnesses were caused by her history of drinking and smoking and some were brought on by the dysautonomia disease. If she ever had pain, no one would know. Pain to Jan was "I don't feel good."

In December 2000, Jan's dysautonomia kicked in. She had no pain but was very weak and in poor health. Mom took her to see the doctor. The nurse practitioner checked her temperature with three different thermometers. Her temperature was eighty-six degrees. The nurse practitioner could not figure out what was wrong with the thermometers. Mom told her there was nothing wrong with the thermometers.

The nurse practitioner said, "If her temperature was 86 degrees she would be dead."

Mom told her, "No, if it were you or I, then yes we would be dead, but not with Jan."

Jan was admitted to the hospital. Her blood sugar had dropped to thirty-six so they gave her an intravenous feeding of 10 percent dextrose for three days to raise her blood sugar to a normal of 70. She became very confused and, being a Houdini, would not stay in bed. She would work her way out of the restraints and go to the bathroom. The nurses were afraid she would fall and hurt herself, so Dad stayed with her all day, since Mom had to care for the residents. At night, the nurses would give her a sleeping pill so she would not try to get out of bed. After a week, she finally recovered and went home. Dad stayed with them for a week until Jan was able to resume her duties in the residential-care facility.

The next December was a repeat of 2000. After being in the hospital again, she decided she should quit smoking. She saw a hypnotist who helped her with the problem, and she successfully quit.

Jan would become angry over anything or nothing. Mom started checking her blood sugar and it would be 50 or below. She would insist Jan eat something. Reluctantly, Jan would eat something and would get over being angry. She would eat her meals but apparently wasn't eating enough to hold her through until the next meal. It got so when Jan felt angry she knew her blood sugar was low and would check it. Sure enough, it would be under 50, so she started keeping candy around for such occasions. Controlling her sugar also seemed to keep her from getting sick. Jan ran the residential-care facility for the elderly for eleven years. In December 2006, due to Jan's health, Mom and Jan gave up their license and closed the facility. Because Winnie had no family of her own and had become like family to Mom and Jan, she continued to live with them and paid rent.

Jan had been going to church with Mom on Sabbath and was rebaptized on December 2, 2006. Some of the little kids in church would stare at Jan, and it really disturbed her. One day, she told one of them to turn around, look at the pastor, and stop looking at her. They continued to gawk at her each week. Mom tried to ease her distress by explaining that they were just kids and didn't understand why her eyes were like they were.

Mom would tell the children's story at church, and one day she told the story of a little girl who had her eyes operated on and was legally blind but was a loving person. She told them how other children treated this girl because they were curious and how they did not realize how they were making this girl feel. I don't know if they got the picture, but their parents must have because they stopped staring at her. Jan also let them know that she liked riding a bike, cooking, and doing ceramics. This helped them to understand that she was a normal person.

Mom bought a home in Grand Junction, Colorado in 2005 so she could retire here. My sons, Linda, and I did a complete remodel on

Mom's house. Jan did not like the idea of leaving Dad behind with no one to look after him, but Mom was at retirement age and had worked hard to be able to enjoy the years she had left.

In the spring of 2007, Jan began having right-sided pain. This pain must have been very excruciating for Jan to even feel pain. Dr Emmet Lee scheduled her for an ultrasound of the gallbladder. Mom came to visit us before the ultra sound was to be done. She was getting ready to go home when her friend Rachel called to tell her Jan was having pain and had called 911. Jan was in the emergency room. Mom called the ER to give them a heads-up about what was going on and, then left Colorado and drove home.

The next day, the doctor on call telephoned Mom and told her they had done the ultrasound and Jan's gallbladder was fine, but the ultrasound showed something wrong with the colon and a lesion on her liver. He wanted to do a colonoscopy. Mom explained to him that what he saw with her colon was the Teflon band that had been put around her colon years before to keep her rectum from prolapsing again. Mom approved him to do a colonoscopy since it had been two years since Jan had one. He also did a biopsy of her liver.

When Dr. Lee returned, he called Mom and told her Jan had been complaining of a headache in the back of her head and he had done a CT Scan to make sure there was no changes to the congenital growth she had there. He also opted to do a CT Scan of her lungs even though the x-rays were clear since she had been a long-time, heavy smoker. He told Mom there was no changes to her head, but her entire right lung was full of cancer. The biopsy of the liver also showed liver cancer that had metastasized from the lungs.

When Jan came home she was weak and could not understand why.

She said to Mom "I thought it was suppose to be the other way around."

Mom asked her what she meant.

She said, "I thought I was supposed to take care of you, instead of you taking care of me." Winnie did what she could to help Jan, but her poor health would not allow her to do much except keep Jan company.

Dori, a friend of Mom's decided to have a pool party and invited some of the people she and Mom worked with. Jan and Winnie went to the party with Mom. Jan enjoyed sitting in the pool but did not have the strength to swim. When Jan started to the car she was so weak Dori and another friend, Larynda had to help her so she would not fall.

Mom had returned to work that spring, and as Jan got progressively worse it was hard for Mom to keep up with it all. On Labor Day weekend, sister Linda went down and got Dad so he could help Mom. Jan was in Hospice care and was slowly deteriorating. Sometimes Dad would put a blanket out on the patio so she could lie in the sun as this was something she always enjoyed.

I've never like funerals, so decided to go see Jan and say my good-bye's while she was alive. Jan knew why I was visiting. To look at her was extremely hard. She weighed about seventy pounds, and her face was basically skeletal. She was on oxygen and was bedridden. It was hard to say good-bye; I didn't know what to say.

She very soon got so weak that the Hospice certified nursing assistant had to give her a bed bath rather than a shower. On October 18, 2007, the Hospice chaplain came at 4:15 p.m. Mom was in Jan's room with him until he started singing, and then Mom stepped out of Jan's room. He left about 4:40 p.m. The registered nurse came at 4:45 p.m. She examined Jan and realized Jan was breathing through her mouth and the oxygen was helping very little if at all. The nurse turned the oxygen from 2 liters up to 4 liters, but it did not help. Dad suggested that maybe they should just take the oxygen off since she was unconscious and the oxygen was doing her no good.

The nurse did just that, and Jan was pronounced at 5:20 p.m. Jan died at fifty-two years of age. She lived forty years longer than doctors had expected and fifteen years longer than anyone had lived with dysautonomia.

Linda and I had five beautiful children. They saw Jan as their caring Aunt. As young children they played with her. Jan would sing as they played. They would laugh but only because what she did or said was funny. She would sing "This Old Man" and other songs you sing in school or church. I have never known any of our children to ever do anything that was unkind to Jan. I have to say that my wife and children are most likely the best example of how our world should treat one another. They are kind and considerate to everyone.

It's too bad that the only way Jan could find her niche in this life was created by our mother. Mom gave Jan the opportunity of a life time, simply because Mom believed in Jan, unlike the rest of us who had given upon her, thinking all she would ever be was a disadvantaged drunk.

I'm here to tell you we need to stop profiling and stereotyping people. Jan proved that every one of us can fit in. We all have our niche in life, in spite of what our ancestors thought and others think today. I myself have hired people who at first glance looked like they couldn't do the job, but given the opportunity, those people adjusted and improvised to make it all happen. We just need to give those people the chance.

After Jan died, the Hospice chaplain came by to see how Mom was handling the grieving process. Jan always loved to sing, and he told Mom that he had sung "Jesus Loves Me" to Jan. He then started to sing "Amazing Grace." These were Jan's two favorite songs. He said Jan had started singing with him and had sung so loudly you would have thought she was singing to the angels. What a blessing that was for Mom to hear.

Jan must have related to John Newton from Olney, England, who wrote the song, because "Amazing Grace" was her favorite. Newton was once an infidel, a libertine, and a dealer of slaves in Africa. By the mercy of the Lord and Savior Jesus Christ he was preserved, restored, pardoned, and appointed to preach the faith that he had long labored to destroy.

When Christ comes, I'm sure Jan will be as perfect as she was the day she was born, and she will no longer be blind but will see. "T'was grace that relieved her fears the hour she first believed."

Mom cut back on her work after Jan's death so she could be with Winnie and care for her. Winnie was a diabetic and also had a rapid heart rate. The doctors put in a pacemaker defibrillator. Winnie died in her sleep one night in April 2008. This was hard for Mom. Then her best friend, Rachel, died; another heartache for Mom. I know Mom loves California, and I'm sure she misses living there and misses my sister Linda and her family. But she is grateful she had bought a house in Grand Junction and has moved here.